Inc.
MAGAZINE
PRESENTS

HOW TO
REALLY
CREATE A
SUCCESSFUL
BUSINESS PLAN

David E. Gumpert

FEATURING THE BUSINESS PLANS OF

PIZZA HUT
SOFTWARE PUBLISHING CORP.
CELESTIAL SEASONINGS
PEOPLE EXPRESS
BEN & JERRY'S

How to Really *Create a Successful Business Plan.*

This publication is designed to provide accurate and authoritative
information in regard to the subject matter covered. It is sold with the
understanding that the publisher is not engaged in rendering legal,
accounting, or other professional service. If legal advice or other expert
assistance is required, the services of a competent
professional should be sought.

Text design by Susan L. Dahl
Cover design by S. Laird Jenkins Corporation

This book is available at special quantity discounts for bulk
purchases for sales promotions,premiums or fund-raising.
Special books or book excerpts can also be created to fit specific needs.
Write: *Inc.* Business Resources, Attn: Special Sales Dept.,
38 Commercial Wharf, Boston, MA 02110-3883 or call 1-800-394-1746.

Library of Congress Catalog Number: 96–77002

ISBN: 1–880394–23–5

Third Edition

1 2 3 4 5 6 7 8 9 10

▼

For Laura, Jason, and Jean

Acknowledgments

EVERY BOOK OF ANY VALUE depends on contributions from individuals other than the author. So it is with this book.

Its value stems from the significant input of five entrepreneurs who graciously agreed to open a part of their past to an outsider's scrutiny. These aren't just any entrepreneurs, but individuals who have started some of America's best-known growth companies.

They are special people because they understand that an important mission of *Inc.* Magazine is to educate. They want to be part of that education process by sharing their experiences—both positive and negative—with other entrepreneurs starting and expanding their businesses.

They had enough confidence in both *Inc.* and in me to allow that scrutiny. For their confidence, *Inc.* and I are very appreciative. So I wish to personally thank these entrepreneurs: Donald Burr, Frank Carney, Fred Gibbons, Mo Siegel, and Ben Cohen. They and their associates have been extremely cooperative and helpful.

Thanks also to Will Taylor, Jan Spiro, Mary Ellen Mullaney, and Stephanie Skinner of *Inc.* for their useful suggestions and feedback. And to my family—wife, Jean, and children Laura and Jason—thank you for your support through this sometimes trying venture.

— *David E. Gumpert*

Table of Contents

NOTE: The business plans are excerpted from real companies and are presented as close to their original forms as possible. In some cases, minor modifications have been made to language and appearance.

PART III.
Completing the Plan

PART IV.
Conclusion

▽

HOW TO

REALLY

CREATE A

SUCCESSFUL

BUSINESS PLAN

Introduction

In recent years, substantial numbers of entrepreneurs have taken to writing business plans. Indeed, there is now statistical evidence about just how many entrepreneurs prepare business plans. Two surveys conducted of business owners during 1993—one sponsored by AT&T and the other by MassMutual—each came out with the same result: 42% of the approximately 500 business owners participating in each survey said they had written a business plan. While the surveys didn't probe into the content of the plans, the simple fact that such a number of business owners now attempts to put plans into writing was surprising to me.

I'd certainly like to think that the first edition of this book, which attracted wide attention, inspired some of the entrepreneurs to write business plans. Regardless, it is gratifying to know that so many business owners have become converts to the idea of doing formal business plans.

Yet even though more business owners seem to be writing plans, I know that the task of writing an effective business plan continues to be a mystery to many entrepreneurs, because they are intimidated by the writing process. This book's purpose is to take the mystery out of business plans and guide executives of smaller growing companies step by step through the process of writing a successful business plan.

A successful business plan is one that focuses your thinking, helps you establish a realistic business strategy, improves your operations, and wins for your company the financing and other support it needs. A proven process exists for writing a successful business plan—whether you are starting a new business or seeking to expand an existing one. To explain that process, this book draws on three principal resources:

1. The experiences of successful entrepreneurs. There's no better way to gain an understanding of what is required for success than to look at how some of the most accomplished entrepreneurs have done it. Drawing on *Inc.* Magazine's reputation and resources, we persuaded the founders of five of America's best-known successful companies to share their business plans with us.

The companies whose business plans are represented include:
- Pizza Hut
- Celestial Seasonings
- People Express
- Software Publishing
- Ben & Jerry's

The book excerpts liberally from the business plans to show exactly how the professionals have done it. It also relies on interviews with the company founders for their insights into the planning process.

2. The experiences of the author in working with entrepreneurs. I have read through dozens of business plans, analyzing their content, advising entrepreneurs on revision, and reworking and rewriting plans so they accomplish the executives' goals. Based on that experience, I have developed a process for assembling successful business plans. It rests on what I call a "building block" approach, in which the planning process moves through specific phases, at the end of which a finished plan results.

3. Exercises and advice. The end of each chapter contains tasks and suggestions for readers to follow up on the analysis presented. The purpose is to involve readers and enable them to see progress in formulating their own business plans. As that happens, the mystery and intimidation of the process vanish.

Writing a business plan is part and parcel of building a successful business. And, as I hope this book demonstrates, writing a business plan can be just as exciting as growing a company.

PART ONE:

PLAYING THE BUSINESS PLAN GAME

CHAPTER ONE:

What Is a Business Plan and Why Should I Write One?

YOU HAVE TO write a business plan. Perhaps your bank has "suggested" that you include a business plan with your loan application. Or potential investors you approached for financing asked for one. Or that financial whiz you're trying to recruit as your company's chief financial officer wants to see one to help decide whether to become a part of your team.

However the request was made, you probably said something like, "Oh, sure. I want to do a little fine-tuning first. Then I'll get it off to you. No problem."

And now you're trying to figure out what to do next. Because you don't have a plan and you don't know how to begin to write one.

I've met hundreds of entrepreneurs in the course of writing about and working with smaller businesses over the past dozen years and, next to the individual facing business failure, none is more poignant than the man or woman who must write a business plan. When he or she tells me about the task ahead, it's usually in a tone of voice not much different from what you would expect if the person were looking ahead to ten years' hard labor in Leavenworth. "Well, I guess I'll just start writing," they usually sigh.

What happens next varies with the individuals. Sometimes they do start writing and invariably come out with something more akin to stream of consciousness than a business plan. More often than not, they get writer's block and find ways to weasel out of the task. They try a different bank or different investors, looking for those who won't ask the awful question. They recruit the financial whiz, marketing genius, or other hot prospect with promises of a business plan down the road.

What Is a Business Plan in Business Terms?

You've probably heard all the academic and formal definitions of a business plan—something to the effect that it's a document describing your company's goals and means of achieving them over the next five years. However it's phrased, though, the definition is usually abstract and uninformative. It makes a business plan sound dry and theoretical—and mysterious—which it is not.

Here's how I define a business plan: *It's a document that convincingly demonstrates that your business can sell enough of its product or service to make a satisfactory profit and be attractive to potential backers.* In other words, a business plan is a *selling document*. It sells your business and its executives to potential backers of your business, from bankers to investors to partners to employees.

Why Bother?

When viewed as a selling document, the business plan takes on a new meaning. This view provides three compelling reasons for writing a business plan:

1. A business plan, first and foremost, should sell *you* on the business.

Fred Gibbons recalls that when he decided to become a

founder of Software Publishing Corp., in 1980, he was about to quit a fast-track job at Hewlett-Packard and take out a second mortgage on his house to help raise $50,000 of start-up funding. He concluded that he needed to write a business plan to confirm the wisdom of those steps. In his words, the plan was his "sanity check."

If you do all the things you're supposed to do in writing a business plan, you may decide at some point in the writing process that the business doesn't make as much sense as you'd anticipated. The market isn't growing as fast as you'd thought or the gross margins aren't as high as you'd expected. And you may decide not to pursue the business. In that event, the business plan has done you a favor—it has saved you the expense and grief of pursuing a business that wasn't really viable.

Conversely, you may discover in the course of researching and writing the plan that the business opportunity isn't exactly what you'd expected, but that if you alter your focus slightly, the opportunity is even greater than you'd realized. You may change your approach to take the new realities into account, making the business more exciting than before.

A manager of a small wholesaler of cut flowers wrote a business plan in response to a demand for one from its chief investor, who was concerned about the company's eroding profits. In doing the research to write a plan, the manager discovered that competitors were devising ways to sell the freshest and prettiest flowers as special premium brands—fetching higher prices than usual. The manager decided to propose to the investor a plan for creating a special inspection and grading system so that interested customers could ensure they were getting the best of the bunch. The investor liked the idea well enough to authorize funding for the project. The new premium-brand project enabled the company to raise its prices to some customers and to attract new ones. Over the next few years, profitability improved significantly, thanks to the effort made in putting together a business plan.

2. A business plan sells others on the business. When someone asks you for a business plan, they are really saying, "Sell me on this business. Turn me on."

In that sense, a business plan is not unlike the marketing materials your company produces. The advertising, direct mail, public relations, and other promotional copy your company puts together is meant to sell your company to potential customers.

A business plan is meant to sell your company as well, but to those we might call "stakeholders." These are individuals and companies considering providing support of some kind, be it funding, time, expertise, or whatever. Usually, they are bankers, investors, executives, suppliers, significant customers, and so on.

3. A business plan gives you confidence. Having gone through the planning process for my own business, I know what a great feeling it is to complete a written business plan. Suddenly, I felt more in control of my business. That feeling of control was really one of confidence. I knew where my business stood and where it was going. I had also established criteria against which to compare my performance a year out. It was a good feeling.

4. A business plan improves your chances of success. I referred in the first paragraph of the introduction to studies of entrepreneurs done by AT&T and MassMutual. In the AT&T study, all the entrepreneurs were asked to rate their overall success. Those 42% who had written business plans rated themselves more successful than the 58% who hadn't written business plans. In other words, planning paid off.

What About the Real World?

All this sounds fine, you say, but surely many successful businesses got started and grew quickly without the benefit of a plan. And indeed, if you talk to highly successful entrepreneurs and ask them how they started their businesses, you discover that a sur-

12

prising number never wrote a business plan. (See the box on page 16.) The next question is obvious. If Frank Carney can start and grow Pizza Hut and Gordon Segal can start and grow Crate & Barrel and Debbie Fields can start and grow Mrs. Fields Cookies without business plans, why can't I start and/or grow ABC Widgets without one? I offer two reasons:

1. Times have changed. When Frank Carney started his company in the 1950s and Gordon Segal and Debbie Fields started theirs in the 1970s, the competitive climate was much less intense than it is now. Only about 100,000 businesses were being incorporated annually during the 1950s and just over 200,000 yearly during the mid-1970s. By the mid-1990s, that number had climbed to more than 600,000 annually. Add to that the increasingly intense competition from foreign and U.S. corporations and it's clear that making it today with your own business is tougher than it has ever been. You need every advantage you can get.

2. Most of us probably aren't as talented as the famous entrepreneurs. I don't mean this as a put-down. It's just that people like Segal and Fields are highly skilled entrepreneurs whose talent compensates for the lack of a business plan. Most of us aren't as fortunate. We need to identify potential problems and opportunities before it's too late to do anything about them.

A Document for All Seasons— and Purposes

How does a business plan sell the business? By allowing the business to exploit the opportunities that arise in the life of a business from start-up to maturity—and are essential to achieve success. A written business plan becomes your company's representative, much as a salesperson or executive serves as its representative during sales and conference presentations and meetings. Here are some of the main ways in which a business plan can serve your company:

1. Obtaining bank financing. For most banks, it's usually enough that an applicant provide past and current financial statements to get a formal hearing for a loan. But in today's world, just getting a hearing isn't enough. Because more companies are seeking bank financing than banks have money available, only those businesses that make the best case will receive funds.

A business plan helps set you apart from the crowd. I've had any number of bankers tell me that while their banks don't require business plans, companies that submit plans immeasurably improve their chances of getting the funds they seek.

Keep in mind that bankers are nervous, averse to risk. A written business plan carries an important message even before it's read: it says the company's executives are serious enough to do formal planning. That's an important message because bankers believe that those individuals who plan are better risks than those who don't, and more deserving of bank funds.

2. Seeking investment funds. Venture capitalists and other investors require a business plan from any company that wants to be taken seriously for funding. It's the first thing most ask for, much as a personnel manager asks job applicants for a résumé. Investors use business plans as a screening device, looking to be turned on to a business with significant growth potential. When something catches their eye, they read more carefully and, if they are still intrigued, they will come back to the executives for further discussion.

3. Arranging strategic alliances. Strategic alliances are arrangements between large and small companies to carry out joint research, marketing, and other activities. They have become more common in the last few years. For small companies, arranging a strategic alliance with a large company can mean gaining access to important financial, distribution, and other resources. But before a large company will even consider a strategic alliance, its executives will want to examine a smaller company's business plan.

4. Obtaining large contracts. Smaller companies seeking to obtain a large chunk of business from a major corporation can encounter a common obstacle. It comes when the corporate representative says something like: "Everyone knows who we are, but very few people know who you are. More important, we don't know whether you'll be around long enough to fill all the obligations we expect for the big bucks we'll be paying you." At this point, producing a business plan can go a long way toward reassuring a corporation.

5. Attracting key employees. For a smaller company going after a top-notch executive, there's usually a two-way diligence process going on. The company wants to be sure the executive is as good as presented and the executive wants to be sure the company is right for his or her talents. A business plan can save a lot of conversation, besides instilling the necessary confidence to snare that hotshot.

6. Completing mergers and acquisitions. Whether you want to sell your company or acquire another one, a business plan can go a long way toward helping you stand out from the crowd. And in today's frenzied merger/acquisition world, that can be very important. When you go to sell your company, you'll be scrutinized by potential buyers who are looking at many companies. One large chemical firm looked at more than 200 companies in its search for a small specialty chemical business to acquire. When it found a company that looked solid, its business plan helped seal the deal.

Frank Carney credits his business plan with helping make Pizza Hut attractive enough that Pepsico eventually acquired it. And Mo Siegel says that Celestial Seasonings' sale to Kraft Foods was due in large measure to the herbal tea company's annually prepared business plan.

Similarly, if you are doing the acquiring, you'll be looking at many companies before you decide to plunge ahead. Should you be in competition to acquire a business, your business plan can once again inspire the confidence essential to completing the deal.

7. Motivating your management team. One of the major problems confronting growing companies is communicating the company's strategy and business approach within the

■ Those Who Didn't Write a Plan And Lived to Laugh About It

When I began writing this book, I called a number of entrepreneurs who had started extremely successful businesses to ask them for copies of their early business plans. I wanted to use excerpts from the plans to illustrate the right way to write a plan. In a surprising number of cases, after I explained my intention, I encountered an uncomfortable silence. Then came a soft laugh, followed by a sheepish explanation: "You won't believe this, but. . . "

Here is how some of the entrepreneurs explained their lack of a written business plan:

• **James Barclay, a founder of Reebok International Inc.** "Our plan was basically to stay alive from month to month," he recalls. For a year after the company started, in 1979, "There was nothing [written] on a formal basis." After a year or so, "We began putting together sales projections to have some idea of what we needed to buy."

By 1981, with the company already past the $1-million sales mark, Reebok received significant funding from a corporate investor that acquired 50% of the company. But even then Reebok didn't have a business plan. The corporation "realized that what held us back [from faster company so everyone is working toward the same goals. When individuals in a small company have different visions about the company's strategy, customers may become confused about what the company is trying to accomplish. A written business plan that is based on input from all members of the company's management team and distributed to all managers ensures that everyone understands where the company is headed. In the process, the plan serves as a motivational tool by laying out the company's financial, marketing, and production goals.

growth] was not having enough product," says Barclay. Today, Reebok does more than $1 billion in annual sales.

• **Randy Fields, a founder of Mrs. Fields Cookies.** "Our company is so strategic in its strength and nature that we don't need a written plan," he says. "Our plan is part of our culture."

The company was founded in 1977 and after 12 years had 8,000 employees scattered around the globe running the company-owned cookie stores—and no business plan. "Everyone knows what the strategy and mission of the company are," says Fields. "Every conversation relates to it. . . . We would trivialize the plan to write it down."

• **Frank Carney, a founder of Pizza Hut**. When Frank and his brother founded the company, in the 1950s, "It was casual. We were in college." By 1970, though, when the company began to grow explosively and went public, "We about lost control of the operations," he says. "Then we figured out that we had to learn how to plan." The result was a written plan that helped the company get back on the growth track.

• **Gordon Segal, founder of Crate & Barrel.** "I'm the worst person in the world to ask about planning," he says. The company has never had a written business plan.

A note of caution: Obviously, you won't show your business plan to every Tom, Dick, and Harry who happens along with a deal of some sort. And even when you do want to show a plan to an outsider, you may want to omit some sensitive information or alter your approach to meet differing reader interests. Moreover, you want to protect proprietary information in the plan from being misused. In Chapters 10 and 11, I look at ways of tailoring your business plan to fit your audience and to reduce the risk of your plan being misused.

Nontraditional applications. Business plans have even begun to be used outside of the business world. Many nonprofit and government organizations now routinely develop written plans to guide their organizations.

The executives of these organizations are coming to the realization that even though their organizations aren't profit-making entities, they must be on sound financial footing and have compelling reasons to continue attracting funds. Nonprofit hospitals, for example, face a tumultuous world of mergers, downsizings, and reorganizations, reflecting a major shake-up in the world of health care.

Even seemingly "safe" organizations, like public schools, are discovering they must plan ahead if they are to survive the rapidly changing world order. Over a two-year period I was involved in an effort by my town's school system to develop a strategic plan. The school's superintendent and school board members are farsighted enough to anticipate the changes being wrought by school choice and new private school competitors.

The planning process is much the same for nonprofit and government organizations as for businesses. These organizations need to develop a strategy, target their markets, focus on product and/or service quality, and attend to all the other matters that a business must consider.

But in addition to business considerations, nonbusiness organizations must pay attention to an additional factor: their governing constituencies. For most small businesses, the governing constituency is the board of directors, which is controlled by the owners. But hospitals, museums, and charities have boards of trustees that control policy-making decisions. A school district has a school board and a town has aldermen, selectmen, or some such variation. The members of these governing bodies may have different agendas and interests than the executives running the organizations on a day-to-day basis. In addition, local agencies often have community-based constituencies—parents for schools, for example. They need to feel they had input into the planning process, via mailed questionnaires, open planning meetings, and other such tools.

Thus, the executives often confront a political challenge in getting the governing constituencies to "buy in" to the planning process. One way or another, the executives must make the governing constituencies feel a part of the planning process or risk having them feel they are being left out of the process. If they feel left out, they may sabotage the planning process or simply ignore any plans that come out of it.

Getting Started: Look Inward

All right, you say. Enough of the arguments. You're convinced you should have a business plan. Now what do you do?

The obvious answer is that you begin planning, but that doesn't really give you much practical guidance. Before you can begin planning a business's goals and objectives, you have to first clarify your own goals and objectives.

Before this begins sounding theoretical, let me point out that what I'm really talking about is determining what you want out of your business life. To make the process worthwhile, I suggest you begin by examining your personal aspirations and objectives.

We tend to equate success with making lots of money. But when you really come down to it, success means being happy doing whatever it is you are spending your time doing. To put it another way, it's hard to be successful financially if you aren't personally satisfied with your work. You just aren't as motivated doing something you don't enjoy doing. To succeed in today's competitive business climate, you have to be highly motivated.

Here are four basic questions to ask yourself to begin determining your personal objectives:

1. What kind of businessperson are you?

• *Are you a "people person" who prefers working with or directing others?* If you welcome the challenges of managing, you'll do best with a growing organization. Keep in mind, though, that directing a rapidly growing organization is much different from operating a small stable business with a handful of employees.

• *Do you prefer to work in a small group or alone?* If you are starting a business primarily to achieve freedom and independence, you may feel more comfortable working with just a few people or even alone. Many entrepreneurs who start companies to avoid having a boss suddenly find that having many subordinates to manage is tougher than any boss was. More and more of these individuals work alone or with just a few employees and love it. The company may be growing slowly, but in a manageable way.

2. Do you want your money now or later?

This may sound like a crazy question, but there are significant differences in how the two types of situations just described tend to pay off for their founders. The small, slow-growing business is likelier to make large amounts of money for its owner sooner than a fast-growing *Inc.* 500 type of business. This too may sound strange, but the latter business requires that most or all of its profits be reinvested to fuel the growth—to pay for new employees, equipment, and office space. In the fast-growth business, you'll probably make your money some years down the road, when the business can afford to pay large salaries and may be ripe for going public or being sold to a major corporation.

3. What kind of business do you want?

I like to separate businesses broadly into two types:

• *Lifestyle businesses.* The title is a bit misleading because it conjures up visions of working at the business in the morning while playing golf in the afternoon. It really applies to the bulk of the nation's millions of small businesses, which have a handful of employees and are growing slowly. These businesses allow their owners to enjoy a lifestyle in which they practice a trade or service they enjoy, have the independence of being the boss, and earn a better living than they ever could at a job.

• *High-flyer businesses.* These are the businesses we're always reading about in *Inc.* and other business publications—the glamorous businesses increasing their sales at 50% to 100% annually, while adding dozens of new employees. Those that can keep the pace up for five years or more may go public or be acquired by major corporations. Those entrepreneurs who are successful starting growth businesses often make it look easy, especially in retrospect.

4. What are your personal goals for the future?

This is one of those difficult questions that most of us would rather avoid. The answer has to do with personal values and preferences. What do you really enjoy doing? Producing your business's product? Selling it? Developing new products or services? And how important are nonbusiness matters? Would you like to spend more time with your family? Travel more? Pursue certain hobbies?

Perhaps most pertinent is the issue of whether you can make your personal goals fit into your business goals, and vice versa. If you want to spend more time with your family, is it possible to involve family members in the business? Or could you run the business from your home so you'll be more available to family members? Or does that desire mean you must reduce the amount of time you spend in the business? If you want to travel more, is it possible to accomplish that goal via selling more of your products and/or services internationally? If you really prefer to develop new products, could you recruit a chief executive to grow the business?

It is helpful to write your goals down. Try to express them both in general terms and specific targets of where you'd like to be in five years. For example, perhaps you'd like to be spending 50% of your time developing new products, or taking one international trip a year, or moving your business from an office to your home.

Clearly, the more closely your personal and business goals match, the happier you'll be. And in my experience, the happier you are, the more enthusiastic you'll be about your business. And the more enthusiastic you are about your business, the more likely you are to succeed.

A note of caution: Keep in mind that the business you want isn't necessarily the business you can have. I recall two entrepreneurs who asked for my help in writing a business plan to raise venture capital for an office supply wholesaling business. While it's certainly possible for such a business to become a high flyer, it's more likely to thrive as a lifestyle business. Alternatively, a high-technology business in certain industries almost has to be a high flyer in order to keep up with the fast growth of its industry.

The Personal Objectives Matching Game

If you write a business plan to show to bankers or potential acquirers, you probably won't include a section on your personal objectives. But answering the questions just posed will make the writing process easier than it might otherwise have been and will lead to a clearer, more focused business plan. That's because you will be pursuing the kind of business you feel most comfortable with. That comfort will translate into enthusiasm and creativity.

You can begin using the questions in your own planning

effort by constructing what I call *The Personal Evaluation Equation.* Here's how it looks:

PERSONAL EVALUATION EQUATION				
Kind of Person		**When Want $$**		**Kind of Business**
Small group	+	Early	=	Lifestyle business
Large group	+	Later	=	Growth business

A few points need to be raised about this little exercise:

1. What if there's a mismatch? Maybe you have the leadership and managerial abilities that would enable you to handle a large group operation, but you want your riches as quickly as possible. You should be asking yourself some tough questions, then, about just what your priorities are. If you conclude that the money can wait, then a growth business may make sense. If not, then perhaps you want to alter your focus to a lifestyle business.

2. Isn't it possible for a lifestyle business to suddenly turn into a growth business, and vice versa? Most certainly. One point to be emphasized about planning in general is that plans don't always work out as expected, either in personal life or business life. Any number of entrepreneurs who thought they were starting a simple lifestyle business have been swept into a growth business by the demands of the marketplace. At the same time, it's important to emphasize that the chances of achieving your goals are much greater if you plan your approach. So don't go starting a lifestyle business and expect that fate will turn it into a growth business.

3. Either path is acceptable. One reason for going through this exercise is to debunk the notion that every entrepreneur has to set his or her sights on being the next Fred Smith or Steve Jobs. Not everyone is equipped to make that happen, nor would everyone who starts a business necessarily enjoy the process involved in making it happen. It's possible to be very successful financially running a one-person business or a small organization of fewer than 25 people.

EXERCISES

Worksheets for this chapter are provided on page 207

To get you started in the planning process, here are two exercises. The first is a quiz and the second is a writing assignment.

I. QUIZ

1. Which do you prefer?
   a. Personally making your business's product or fulfilling its service.
   b. Getting others to do the work.

2. What kind of organization interests you more?
   a. A small, stable organization.
   b. A fast-growing organization with lots of new people and new assignments.

3. Which approach to work gives you the most satisfaction?
   a. Doing detailed tasks such as personally keeping the books.
   b. Making strategic decisions but getting others to execute them.

4. Which leadership style best describes you?
   a. Like to be in charge of the business.
   b. Am willing to share authority with others.

5. Which of these business goals are most important to you?
   a. Achieving the freedom and independence of being the owner.
   b. Gaining the satisfaction of seeing the organization grow and expand.

6. Which of the following financial goals is most important to you?
   a. Making a good living from the business within three years.
   b. Making a marginal living from the business for several years, with the prospect of becoming a millionaire in seven to ten years.

7. How do you feel about hiring and motivating people?
   a. It's one of the business tasks an owner has to endure.
   b. It's one of the great challenges and sources of excitement in running a business.

If you picked five or more "a" answers, you're a good candidate for a lifestyle business. If you picked five or more "b" answers, you're a good candidate for a high-flyer business.

II. WRITING ASSIGNMENT

Describe in 50 words or less your principal personal goals in starting, operating, or expanding your business.

Previewing the Business Plan: The Best Type for You

WHEN I SPEAK with entrepreneurs who are embarking on writing a business plan, I begin by asking them some of the questions I included at the end of the last chapter. What do you personally want from the business? What kind of business are you most comfortable with? What do you do best?

As they consider such questions, they invariably have inquiries of their own. What should the business plan look like? How should it be arranged? What should be included in each section? How long should it be?

In other words, as they begin the planning process, they also want to have a vision of the plan. They want to know what blanks they're going to have to fill in. That's understandable, and to help in that process this chapter offers some introductory answers to those questions. To illustrate different approaches to writing and organizing business plans, the chapter includes some contents pages and excerpts from the business plans of several successful well-known companies.

Before running through the components of a business plan, let's look at some basic principles of business plans:

1. There's no one right way to organize and write a business plan. Writing a business plan is as much art as science. As you'll see in the comparisons of contents pages and opening sections from the business plans of Software Publishing, People Express, and Celestial Seasonings later in this chapter, business plans can differ widely in organization and contents. Moreover, fill-in-the-blank computer software programs for business plans have recently become available. I'm not too keen on these, for the reasons explained in the box on page 33.

2. You can be creative in the business plan's packaging and presentation as long as you know the limitations of creativity. It's fine to use the marvels of desktop publishing and graphics to package your business plan attractively. Indeed, I provide some ideas in Chapter 11 for jazzing up the appearance of your business plan in ways that can improve its selling effectiveness. But there are certain subjects—for instance, financial results and projections—that demand conformity with the tried-and-true.

3. Keep the plan as concise and focused as possible. You may feel your business is so complex that a plan requires long sentences, big words, and many pages of explanation. However, it's essential to make the plan as accessible as possible if it is going to be of maximum use. The plan must be both complete and easy to read and understand.

4. Make sure the plan captures your company's energy and personality. Every business has, or should have, its own special character that includes an excitement about and commitment to its markets and products or services. I'm talking about more than enthusiasm and confidence. I'm referring to the sense of purpose that sets the company and its people apart from competitors. As much as possible, the business plan should capture this special outlook and sense of purpose.

5. Be sure to include negatives as well as positives. It's natural when writing a business plan to do what you do in sales and promotional pitches—talk only about the great things the company does. But to be credible, the business plan must acknowledge and discuss the industry and company weaknesses that are a part of every business, no matter how successful.

6. Write the business plan over a period of weeks. Few credible business plans are written over a weekend. The business plan must evolve over several weeks, and sometimes even months, to reflect the array of challenges and opportunities facing the business. However, letting the process drag on too long may mean the plan never gets completed.

What All Plans Must Cover

Here is a brief overview of the contents of the written plan. Keep in mind that after the first two items, the titles of the subsequent sections can vary. But every business plan should cover the subjects addressed in this overview:

• **Cover Page.** On the cover page goes the name of your company, its address and phone number, and the chief executive's name. That may seem obvious, but it's amazing how many business plans don't have a cover page or have an incomplete one. Nothing will turn off a banker or investor faster than having to look up your telephone number in the phone book because you left it off the cover page. Moreover, if the plan is going to be distributed to several bankers or investors, you will want to number each plan prominently on the cover page—to allow you to track the plans and to inhibit recipients from copying or widely passing around the plan. (You should also have recipients sign a nondisclosure statement, which is discussed in Chapter 11.)

• **Table of Contents.** This should include a logical arrangement of the sections of your business plan, with page numbers. Once again, this is something that seems obvious, but many business plans are put together with content pages and no page numbers.

- **Executive Summary.** This is the heart of the business plan. It is so important to both the preparation and final effectiveness of the plan that it merits its own separate chapter. (See Chapter 4.)

- **The Company.** The business plan must provide basic information about the company: its past, present, and future. That is, there should be information about the company's history or, if it's a start-up, about the evolution of the market and product concept. Information is necessary as well about the company's current status. And what is the company's future strategy? What are its goals and what actions are required to achieve its goals?

- **The Market.** This is your assessment of the customer groups you've targeted, other customer groups you might pursue, the competition, and marketing efforts thus far. Is the market growing, how fast is it growing, and what evidence do you have that it is interested in your product or service?

- **The Product/Service.** Here is where you describe your product and/or service and what makes it special and attractive. What are the components of the product/service? How much do you charge? What services don't you provide? What kind of warranty do you provide and what are its particular provisions?

- **Sales and Promotion.** This is your assessment of how you intend to carry out your marketing plan—how you'll reach your customers and sell to them. Do you have an in-house sales force or will you use manufacturer's representatives, direct mail, or contracted telemarketers to sell your product/service? What kind of public relations do you have planned? Will it be done internally or will you hire a public relations firm?

- **Finances.** Here is where you detail your past results, if there are any, and your expectations for the future. This section should include cash flow projections, profit-and-loss statements, and balance sheets. All the figures should be cast in traditional accounting format, which is discussed in detail in Chapter 9.

CHAPTER TWO

Keep in mind. . . The order of the subjects listed here is not random; they are given in order of importance. It is no accident that information about markets comes before information about products/services. You'll be reading lots more about the importance of marketing over and above any other single subject.

Mold the Business Plan to Your Needs

As I've indicated, there's more than one way to write a business plan. Indeed, there are infinite variations on the theme. The only thing that really counts is if the plan does what it's supposed to do: sell you and others whose support you need.

I've seen all kinds of business plans in my years of working with smaller companies, ranging from three-page summaries to tomes of well over 100 pages. I believe that entrepreneurs should have some sense of how long and elaborate the business plan will be before they begin writing. To help in that task, I've categorized business plans into three main types. I've also included an example for each category of a well-known company's plan to show how the plan is put together and what it covers:

1. The Summary Business Plan: The Software Publishing Model

The summary business plan is a business plan in short form. It contains the most important information about a business and its direction, minus important supporting detail. A summary plan is usually 10 to 15 pages long and is concise and even terse in style.

The original business plan for Software Publishing Corp., the Mountain View, Calif., maker of PFS Software for IBM PCs, provides an excellent illustration of a summary plan. It is 10 pages long and, as can be seen in the first two pages reproduced in Exhibit 2–1, is quite terse. The Business Strategy is stated in one sentence. Note that the first two pages focus on marketing issues rather than product issues. Indeed, more than half the plan deals with marketing issues: pricing, competition, and distribution channels.

Generally speaking, summary business plans work best in the following situations:

1. You're applying for a bank loan. Since most bankers don't officially require a business plan, a summary plan will likely both impress them and supply the facts they're looking for, especially if it emphasizes past and future financial results.

2. You're well known. If you've previously started a successful business or come from a prominent company, potential investors may be satisfied with a summary plan. In one case, I worked with an AT&T executive who was well known in a specialized technology and was seeking funding for a new business he was starting with some other executives at the company. Because of the prominence of both his company and his scientific work, he opted to write a summary plan and succeeded in attracting investment funds.

In the case of PFS Software, the founders came from Hewlett-Packard, where they had established excellent reputations in the software field. They were a known commodity and succeeded in raising venture capital funds.

3. You're starting a lifestyle business. If you're not seeking outside funding, then a summary business plan may be all that's necessary to convince you and your partners of the validity of what you plan. You might also want to use the plan to persuade relatives or friends to invest a few thousand dollars each, if such funding is necessary.

4. You want to gauge investor interest. You may want to give potential investors a summary plan as a prelude to providing a full plan. Those interested in having more details about the business may request a full plan. Of course, that means you must have two business plans, which isn't as onerous as it sounds, since my approach to writing and tailoring the business plan—considered in Chapters 3, 10, and 11—involves several stages and can be adapted to writing a summary and full plan.

5. Speed is of the essence. In some cases, the market is moving so quickly and the opportunity is so pressing that there's simply not enough time to prepare a full-length business plan. Certainly this was part of the challenge facing Software Publishing in 1981, with the PC revolution just under way and developing at almost breathtaking speed.

2. The Full Business Plan: The People Express Model

If there's such a thing as a standard business plan, the full business plan is it. It's usually a 30- to 50-page document with from 10 to 30 pages of supporting documentation (résumés of key executives, letters from satisfied customers, promotional material, and so forth).

When properly executed, the full business plan is at once loaded with detail and concise. It provides enough information to understand and assess the business properly, but not so much as to be unwieldy. It must answer basic business questions, yet also be flexible in its format.

The People Express business plan (see Exhibit 2–2) well illustrates a full business plan. From the table of contents we see that its organization is unusual (and can be criticized for lacking page numbers). The executive summary comes at the end rather than at the beginning of the plan. It is also tailored to the airline industry.

In comparing the People Express introduction (see Exhibit 2–2) with the Software Publishing one, it's apparent that the former is more detailed, more explanatory. It concentrates on the environmental changes that made a discount airline attractive—deregulation, absence of unions, and high value of used jets, for example. The format allows People Express's founders to provide examples for their points.

Because the airline's founder, Donald Burr, was already well known in the airline business thanks to his visibility as a senior officer at Texas International Airlines Inc., you may wonder why he didn't just do a summary plan. He faced the challenge of explaining a new, unfolding, and complex set of business conditions to potential investors. A summary plan would probably not have done the business concept he was proposing and promoting justice.

The full business plan works best in these situations:

1. You want to explore and explain the business's key issues fully. Few businesses can be explained adequately in ten pages or so, especially if there are innovations in the marketing, production, or other functions. And to be successful today, it's almost a prerequisite that businesses are doing at least one or two innovative things.

2. You're seeking a substantial amount of financing. If you're looking for more than $500,000 of investment funds, the potential backers will want the kind of detail about your company that can be explained only in a full business plan. For that kind of money, it can be argued, they're entitled to a detailed explanation of your company's situation.

3. You're looking for a strategic partner. A major corporation will also likely want the kind of detail that can be found only in a full business plan.

3. The Operational Business Plan: The Celestial Seasonings Model

This is the internal planning document of an operating company. It is developed from the input of key executives and provides a common focus for top managers.

In examining the Celestial Seasonings operating plan for 1984, a few things become quickly apparent:

• At 135 pages, it is much longer than the full business plan. I would venture that this plan could be shortened considerably. But it does take more space to describe and plan a substantial, ongoing business than it does a start-up or small young company. There's more history, more products, and more people.

• It's heavy on quantitative analysis (Internal Situation Analysis Summary, Gap Analysis, Controls).

• It's inspirational. Part of its intent is to mobilize managers to a common purpose. Thus, there's material on "overarchingc values" and "beliefs." The introductory material shown here is from Celestial Seasonings' Overarching Values (see Exhibit 2–3).

The operational business plan is best for the following situations:

1. The company is growing quickly. The operational plan helps key managers get a handle on where the company is headed and what's expected of them as individuals. The plan helps to give order to the growth.

2. It will be used as part of an annual process. The operational plan may set five-year goals, but ideally it should be updated once a year, as managers reevaluate the company's plans and determine how well the company has been doing versus previous targets.

Keep in mind. . . You should feel comfortable with the type of plan you choose. You may think that a summary business plan is what you want to write because it is shortest and therefore should be easiest. But if you're expecting to raise a lot of investment capital and aren't well known in your industry, a summary plan may not be enough.

EXERCISES

Worksheets for this chapter are provided on page 209

As you come to some decisions about which of these three types of business plans you will write, do the following:

1. ***Begin mapping a table of contents.*** Consider what subjects must be covered in your plan. Evaluate the subject areas listed earlier in this chapter and decide how you should cover them in your business plan. What particular areas must be added to allow you to discuss the special aspects of your industry, as in the People Express model?

2. ***Start to make notes under each subject of your contents.*** As you begin thinking about the subject areas, make a few notes about issues you want to be sure to cover, such as names of competitors (in the section on marketing) or your arguments for having an in-house sales force (in the section on sales).

The process of writing a business plan is just that, a process. Scribbling notes, rearranging things, and adding points over a period of days or weeks is quite helpful. Because, all of a sudden, you're writing.

EXHIBIT 2-1:

FINANCING PROPOSAL:
SOFTWARE PUBLISHING CORP.

**Financing Proposal for
Software Publishing Corp.**

Attached is the executive summary of a business plan for a new venture called "Software Publishing Corp." in the personal computer market. SPC's business objective is to become the leading independent software developer and publisher for personal computers. To achieve this objective SPC is seeking $250,000 in additional equity financing to achieve sales of $.5M, $2M, and $5M in 1981, 1982, and 1983 respectively.

The market for personal computer software is projected by Creative Strategies Inc. to reach $350M by 1983 and continue to grow to over $1 billion by the late 1980s. SPC will build a leadership position in this market by first creating through in-house development a family of information management software designed for personal use by business and professional people. The first product in the family called PFS, a forms-oriented personal filing system for APPLE Computers, is being marketed worldwide today. During the period of 1981 through 1983 SPC will introduce at least two new products per year on APPLE Computers and at least one other hardware base such as ATARI, Commodore, or Hewlett-Packard.

Having created this industry leading product line, SPC will be in a visible and strong position to attract authors and enter the publishing business. This activity is expected to begin in 1982 and offer significant potential for financial return above the $5M sales and 35+% pretax profits forecasted for 1983.

SOFTWARE PUBLISHING CORP.
continued

Business Objective: To develop and market in high-volume quality software at low cost (less than $100 per package) for personal computers which allows individuals to solve their information management problems in a simple and versatile way without programming.

Market Strategy: Software Publishing Corp. is positioning itself as the leading independent software supplier for personal computers by producing products aimed at the fastest-growing segment of the personal computer market: Business/Professional applications. SPC's unique strength in this segment is its ability to produce software which turns the personal computer into a versatile problem-solving tool that individuals can use to describe and solve a problem in their own unique way without programming. By removing the barrier of programming, SPC products will make a unique and needed contribution to the growing market for personal computers.

    The personal computer research report from Data Quest forecasts the sales of personal computers for Business/ Professional applications as follows:

	1981	1982	1983	1984	growth
Total Units (000's)	385	805	1335	1590	41%
Total Sales ($000,000)	$790	$1047	$1307	$1630	33%

During 1980 the leading manufacturers were Tandy (Radio Shack), Apple, Commodore, Atari, and Texas Instruments with market shares of 47%, 23%, 18%, 1%, and 1% respectively. Using

SOFTWARE PUBLISHING CORP.
continued

Creative Strategies Research Report "Very Small Business Computers," the software value of the market is as follows:

	1981	1982	1983	1984	growth
Total Software ($000,000)	$170	$250	$348	$481	41%

No estimates are available as to how these software sales are divided between the system manufacturers and independent software suppliers. As an approximation, minicomputer applications software sales are estimated at 10% from the manufacturers and 90% from independent software companies.

EXHIBIT 2-2:
PEOPLE EXPRESS: CONTENTS AND INTRODUCTION

FROM THE BUSINESS PLAN OF ★ PEOPLE EXPRESS ★

TABLE OF CONTENTS

INTRODUCTION

People Express, Skytrans, or Sundance (the company) are possible names for a new company formed to provide low-cost, high-frequency air transportation service. The new company would be organized and managed in a creative and innovative fashion to generate very high levels of efficiency in the production of airline seats. The efficient production of very low-cost seats makes possible very low prices. Low prices and high quality in terms of high frequency and basic service will generate very high rates of return on equity. The experience of Southwest Airlines, other new airlines, well-managed old airlines, and the principals' recent experience at Texas International indicate that well more than adequate rates of return on equity are readily available. Furthermore, those returns have been historically available without the highly leveraged opportunity that is now available. The combined leverage of management innovation with assets, systems, revenues, and financial management is very powerful. Also, the current political, governmental, and economic environment is favorable to the development of these innovations. A further favorable aspect in the use of new management methods is a new company setting which avoids all the costs and delays of unlearning. Finally, it should be noted that the underlying earning assets can achieve annual cash generation of two to three times their purchase price. Very-low price, high-frequency service is projected to begin June 1, 1981, among cities within 1,000 miles of each other in the Eastern third of the country.

Due largely to the passage of landmark legislation, the Airline Deregulation Act of 1978, a new era of change has enveloped the airline transportation business. After the barnstorming days of the 1920s, the airline industry took hold and grew under a careful monitoring and highly restricting governmental hand. That 40-year period of development led to a very safe, highly protected, high cost, low service environment with inherent competitive complications. These difficulties and costs were masked until recently by the existing governmentally inspired monopoly, better known as route and rate regulation. With the passage of the Deregulation Act, these rules of operation, their associated costs, and frequently the management teams, all of which had been institutionalized over the 40-year period, were now largely if not wholly obsoleted in one sweep. This development, as might be expected, has led to a new period of bubbling and ferment in the air transportation business.

Management will be the key to effectively utilizing this different and more expansive environment to devise new and more efficient methods of transporting people. The management of the proposed company has been in the forefront of the changing industry environment and has generally been regarded to have led the industry in operating and marketing innovations over the past several years. However, the process of developing greater efficiency in the production of seat miles, while well underway, has a long way to go.

High degrees of operating leverage are available to management in several areas. First, the industry's well-known labor and capital intensity can be favorably affected by more aggressive asset utilization techniques. For example, because all employees are new, there is an opportunity through very careful selection and extensive training, to achieve a level of cross-utilization and ownership which will lead to very high levels of ASM's per employee. On the equipment side of the asset ledger, a similar effect can easily be obtained through more aggressive acquisition and usage techniques of the basic earning assets. It is also clear that other hard assets can be similarly squeezed.

Second, new and more efficient methods of delivering the product or new ways of doing business are now available through better use of data processing, analysis, and applied operations research. For example, the whole into-airport-into-plane process can be modified for customer convenience and lowered processing costs.

Third, tremendous and perhaps the most significant leverage resides in service innovations, most particularly in the areas of pricing and frequency, but also in such hassle-prone and customer-dissatisfaction areas as baggage service. These marketing opportunities are nearly limitless, as the whole range of retail merchandising has now become available to air transportation. The leverage is clearly in the revenue implications of these very available marketing innovations.

Fourth, financial leverage has become a well-accepted business fact of life in air transportation largely, of course, due to the excellent collateral of the primary underlying assets which are prodigious cash generators. It would certainly be reasonable to expect an adequate financial structure to take maximum advantage of these possibilities for a heightened return on equity.

Finally, a disciplined approach to the available operating economies, the wide-open opportunities for better employee development, and the clear field for innovation lend themselves well to marketing creativity in presenting this product to the public, all apart from the inherent power of the significant price advantage.

EXHIBIT 2-3:

CELESTIAL SEASONINGS:
OVERARCHING VALUES

From the Business Plan of ★Celestial Seasonings★

From Mo Siegel's personal computer

"There are positive opportunities to be achieved today!"

CELESTIAL SEASONINGS' OVERARCHING VALUES

The following values dictate the actions of Celestial Seasonings management under most conditions. These values are basic principles that our business is built upon and, in combination with the beliefs and mission statement of the company, these should be clear guides of conduct.

1. The superior quality of our botanical products, in combination with superior packaging, is the greatest key to our success.
2. Our love of customers and consumers is manifested by selflessly serving them with a wholehearted dedication in filling their needs in a personal and excellent way.
3. Our commitment to the dignity of the individual is based on our belief that the following priorities in a person's life must be honored: A. GOD first; B. FAMILY second; C. CAREER third.

Preparation Rules: Behind the Scenes with the Experts

FRED GIBBONS wrote Software Publishing Corp.'s business plan by himself over a period of a few weeks. "I had the vision in my head and I put it down," says Gibbons. "Then I double-checked with my team about its reasonableness. They owned it but I was the doer."

Donald Burr worked with two partners to write People Express's business plan; each partner wrote and rewrote various sections, based on their discussions. The plan was started in early January 1980 and completed a month later. "Writing the plan was a fairly painful process," says Burr. "You have to be precise. You have to have numbers that hang together. I'd rather buy planes and hire people."

Pizza Hut's first business plan was written by eight of the company's top executives over a period of three months in 1970. The officials met in four two-day segments to hammer out the details, and it wasn't very pretty, recalls Frank Carney, the company's co-founder and then president. "The first time around was just brutal," he says. "Most managers like to do things. They can't understand why you have to sit around and talk about it."

The process was even more painful for Celestial Seasonings' first business plan, written in 1976, recalls founder and then-president, Mo Siegel. He involved all middle-level and senior-level managers in a process of writing and rewriting; the meetings took at least ten days. "I lost a lot of people over the planning, including a partner," says Siegel. "He hated planning" and couldn't accept all the effort that Siegel put into it. As these experiences demonstrate, there's no one accepted way to write a business plan. Sometimes one of the founding entrepreneurs single-handedly writes the plan. In other cases, a dozen or more top company officials may get involved in a process that stretches out over days of seemingly interminable meetings.

By taking a look at the experiences of the entrepreneurs whose business plans are represented in this book, it's possible to gain some insights into workable approaches for preparing the business plan. This chapter considers a few rules of thumb that emerge from their business planning experiences and explores their individual efforts.

How Your Business Situation Helps Shape Your Plan

Not only does the process of writing a business plan differ from situation to situation, but so does the plan's final form. The rules of thumb described here may seem obvious, but I know from experience that they aren't obvious to the uninitiated.

1. The earlier in the company's history the plan is written, the simpler the process. This isn't to say that it's easy to write a plan for a start-up or early-stage company, only that it's simpler than doing so for an established growing business. As Fred Gibbons points out, he was able to write the business plan, get his partners to agree, and everything was done. Mo Siegel, on the other hand, waited until Celestial Seasonings was six years old and had about $30 million in sales before he wrote the first business plan. He suddenly had many people involved in a lengthy and frustrating process that caused one of his partners to leave the company.

2. The earlier in the company's history the plan is written, the simpler the actual plan. Software Publishing's business plan is ten pages long, in large measure because, "It's for a single product and market" and the company had only four partners, says Gibbons. A subsequent plan, prepared in anticipation of several products and markets, was two or three times longer, he notes. Celestial Seasonings' plan stretches to 135 pages, because the company has about a dozen products and several hundred employees.

3. The plan's purpose helps shape the content. A business plan aimed at obtaining financing for a start-up will contain different information than a plan intended to guide the strategy and operations of a growing multimillion-dollar company. In the former situation, the audience and its needs are well defined, and the business plan can be sharply focused. In the latter situation, the business plan must address all the constituencies that make up a growing company, including the marketing, sales, production, and finance people. These individuals need to understand both what is expected of the company as a whole and what is expected of their individual areas—a more detailed plan is thus needed.

4. The first business plan is the toughest. That's because the process is new and intimidating. But as Frank Carney reports, subsequent business plans that Pizza Hut's management put together were much less stressful, if not necessarily less time-consuming; with experience, the managers became more comfortable with the planning and writing process.

5. It usually helps to involve your management team. A good way to do this is to assign each manager a section of the plan to write. When you see the drafts, you invariably find that their perspectives and your perspective are miles apart. That's frustrating, but it's also useful because you learn where the important differences are and what you need to do to get everyone on a common course.

Keep in mind. . . In writing the plan, you'll invariably take two steps forward and one step back. It's an uneven path, fraught with unforeseen frustrations and difficulties. Thrashing out those difficulties is a key part of the planning process.

**Settling Key
Start-up Issues:
The People
Express
Experience**

The People Express business plan is notable for its lack of emphasis on marketing issues. After all, in early 1980 the idea of a discount airline was new and little tried. Who could be sure that consumers would flock to a new airline that offered cut-rate fares?

But according to Burr, the founders had little concern about that issue. "We felt that a $23 price would blow the market open," he says. He points out that at Texas International, he had been involved in pioneering off-peak fares and, "When we cut prices to the bone, we were full."

Where to locate. Other issues were paramount in the minds of the founders, including where to locate the new company's hub—its base and the place where all flights eventually passed through. Newark, N.J., was first on their list because the airport seemed to be underutilized and was smack in the middle of one of the nation's most densely populated marketplaces. "We talked about Baltimore, Hartford, New Haven, Oakland, and Kansas City," Burr recalls. Oakland in particular intrigued them because its airport also seemed to be underutilized and was located in an attractive market. But PSA was already well established in California. In addition, PSA was, according to Burr, "a better-run carrier than you tended to find in the East."

So they always came back to Newark. "We couldn't understand why an airport of that size in the largest air market in the world wasn't being used," he says. The founders did what they should have done in that situation—they asked around in the industry and did some research. Says Burr: "We decided it was prejudice. Everyone saw Newark as a loser. Other airlines had invested in other places."

Gradually, he says, "We overcame our concern about Newark." The founders even decided that their earlier concerns about living in New Jersey were probably unfounded as well.

How many planes? The business plan calls for the new company to acquire three jets. But within weeks of the plan's completion, that matter became an issue of intense debate as Burr became aware of efforts by several airlines to sell used jets at what he considered attractive prices. Since the country was in a recession at the time, these companies needed cash and were eager to reduce their fleets. Lufthansa, for instance, was willing to sell several Boeing 737s for $3.7 million apiece, which Burr calls "a gift."

Burr wanted to take advantage of a federal aircraft loan program in existence at that time: new airlines could borrow bank funds for the purchases and the government would guarantee 100% of the principal and 90% of the interest. Because the banks could lose very little even if the airline failed, they were willing to make such loans. Within weeks, the plan was modified to allow for the acquisition of 10 planes, and within three months it went up to 14 planes.

The three partners disagreed about the plan's changes. According to Burr, one partner "thought we were wildly optimistic" to believe the new airline could fill 14 planes. Before the end of that year, Burr had engineered the acquisition of 17 planes. The company had also raised $250,000 of venture capital from Citicorp Venture Capital—not a huge amount of money in and of itself, but from a source that gave the company credibility. That credibility made possible an initial public offering in November that raised $23.5 million. Notes Burr, "The rest is history."

**A Logical
Planning Agenda:
The Pizza Hut
Experience**

For the 12 years after Pizza Hut was founded in 1958, its only formal planning consisted of putting together yearly budgets. In 1969, recalls Carney, "We got in trouble."

In an effort to broaden its base of operations in order to position itself to go public, the company acquired 40% of its franchise operations, or 120 stores, to go with the 6 company-owned outlets it already had. Recalls Carney, "We acquired 33 different accounting systems. It took us eight months to get to one."

In the meantime, revenues flattened and profits tumbled. A hastily developed weekly profit reporting system solved the immediate problem, but Carney decided the time had come for additional action, so he took an American Management Association course, "The Management Course for Presidents." In early 1970, Carney began the Pizza Hut planning process by assembling the top officials who reported to him as CEO.

Setting a mission and philosophy. "We would closet ourselves for two days at a time," he recalls. "We did this four times during a three-month period." At the end of the eight days, the company had a plan that was good for a year.

Carney started with the company's mission. "One guy can write the mission in ten minutes," he notes. "But to get everyone committed to the same thing takes about half a day." As the 1977 Pizza Hut business plan notes, "Only when we fully understand the basic concept of our business can we then proceed to establish priorities, strategies, and plans" (see Exhibit 3–1).

The company's mission in 1977 was simply "to increase our share of the pizza market and be a leader in the food service industry."

Once the mission was hashed out, Carney turned to the company's "philosophy." That took another two hours or so of discussion. "The first day was frustrating because we spent the whole day on the mission and philosophy." (For the mission and philosophy the company adopted in 1977, see Exhibit 3–1.)

Identifying weaknesses. While settling on the company's mission and philosophy was tedious, coming to grips with its weaknesses was painful, especially for Carney. Indeed, the process occupied an important part of the planning effort. He recalls one session during the first planning effort with his managers at which they listed more than 45 weaknesses on a blackboard.

Carney had hired a facilitator for that session, who asked Carney not to attend a subsequent session focused on listing additional weaknesses. "I told him that my people wouldn't be afraid to say something in my presence. But I agreed to stay out. When I walked back in after an hour, there were 70 weaknesses listed." Among the weaknesses cited, he says, was a group of beliefs about the company that the managers thought Carney and his brother (also a founder) held. It turned out that those weren't true, and Carney had a chance to straighten matters out.

But, he concludes, "All the weaknesses don't come out until the CEO is out of the room for part of the session." The development of the mission and philosophy and the analysis of weaknesses and strengths leads naturally to the development of a strategy and, finally, to realistic financial projections, says Carney. "That thinking process has to be in all plans."

Setting Appropriate Goals: The Celestial Seasonings Experience

Mo Siegel started Celestial Seasonings in 1970, but didn't put together the company's first real business plan until 1976. Once he began the process, he became involved with a vengeance.

While the process at Celestial Seasonings was similar to that at Pizza Hut, Siegel introduced a few wrinkles. One of the most important was something he calls "Gap Analysis."

Gap analysis is a technique intended to force managers to stretch their thinking about where new growth is going to come from. "I can have 25 plans that say we need to beef this up and we need to beef that up. But the real question is, if you need to grow, do you have the programs to fill your needs?"

Underlying this question is Siegel's assumption that if you simply continue doing what you were doing the prior year, you'll lose 10% or more of sales. That's because the competition will be coming up with ways to take business away from you and there'll be inevitable attrition. In addition, if you plan to increase your sales by, say, 20%, you can't assume that all your plans will come to pass. Indeed, they seldom do.

So if you expect to increase your sales by 20%, you have to allow for decline on one end and the failure to accomplish everything you expected on the other—in other words, you have to "fill the gap" with the sales sources, as Siegel explains it.

Exhibit 3–2 shows Celestial Seasonings' gap analysis for 1984. The company in 1983 had sold 2,257,000 units and was looking to increase to 2,600,000 units in 1984. In the analysis, the company allows, for instance, for a decrease of 100,000 units lost in declining health food business. To fill the gap, it sees possible increases from international sales, advertising, and food service and nonfood accounts.

Gap planning is essential, says Siegel, because it "forces you to do more and think bigger."

EXERCISES

Worksheets for this chapter are provided on page 211

1. Based on the stage of your business and the management team in place, determine who will be involved in drafting and finalizing the business plan.

2. Set aside time for the people involved to write and discuss the business plan.

3. Based on the complexity of your business, set a maximum length for the business plan.

EXHIBIT 3-1:

PIZZA HUT MISSION AND PHILOSOPHY

FROM THE BUSINESS PLAN OF PIZZA HUT

THE MISSION OF PIZZA HUT, INC. IS

to increase our share of the pizza market and be a leader to the food service industry.

THE PHILOSOPHY OF P.H.I. IS TO ACHIEVE EXCELLENCE IN OUR RELATIONS WITH. . .

Customers
By consistently producing customer satisfaction through a high level of service, product quality, cleanliness, and appropriate atmosphere at an acceptable price/value relationship.

Employees
By providing equal opportunity, a climate conducive to a high degree of personal development, a high degree of economic satisfaction, and an opportunity for personal involvement of all employees.

Franchisees
By providing services, products, and systems to optimize the profit potential of our franchisees while ensuring mutual respect through full disclosure of the objectives in the relationship.

Social Environment
By recognizing our social and local community responsibility and encouraging positive involvement.

Stockholders
By initiating action in the best interest of the stockholders and providing a fair return on stockholder's equity consistent with the demands of the marketplace.

Supplier/ Associate Groups
By dealing fairly and ensuring mutual respect through full disclosure of the objectives and the relationships.

EXHIBIT 3-2:

CELESTIAL SEASONINGS:
1984 GAP ANALYSIS

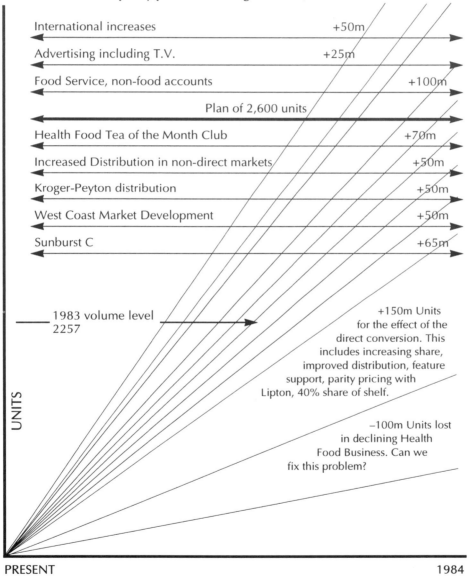

**Celestial Seasonings' Success =
quality products + filling customer/consumer needs**

International increases +50m

Advertising including T.V. +25m

Food Service, non-food accounts +100m

Plan of 2,600 units

Health Food Tea of the Month Club +70m

Increased Distribution in non-direct markets +50m

Kroger-Peyton distribution +50m

West Coast Market Development +50m

Sunburst C +65m

1983 volume level
2257

+150m Units
for the effect of the
direct conversion. This
includes increasing share,
improved distribution, feature
support, parity pricing with
Lipton, 40% share of shelf.

−100m Units lost
in declining Health
Food Business. Can we
fix this problem?

UNITS

PRESENT

1984

Using the Executive Summary as a Guiding Light

A S THE EXPERTS made clear in Chapter 3, there's no one right way to go about writing a plan. One of the most effective approaches I've discovered is to begin by writing an executive summary.

Certainly the most significant part of any business plan is its executive summary. So vital is a good executive summary to a business plan that I'm tempted to wax eloquent about its literary merit.

What *is* an executive summary? Probably the best way to begin defining it is to explain what it *isn't*.

The executive summary is *not* an abstract of the business plan.

The executive summary is *not* an introduction to the business plan.

The executive summary is *not* a preface.

The executive summary is *not* a random collection of highlights.

Rather, the executive summary is *the business plan in miniature.* The executive summary should stand alone, almost as a kind of business plan within the business plan. It should be logical, clear, interesting—and exciting. A reader should be able to read through it in four or five minutes and understand what makes your business tick. After reading your executive summary, a reader should be prompted to say, "So *that's* what those people are up to."

The executive summary should be no more than two pages long. The farther it goes past that point, the less it qualifies as an effective executive summary.

If capturing an entire business in two pages or less sounds like a tall order, it is. In fact, it is probably the most difficult part of the plan to write.

That's because it's usually more difficult to write concisely than it is to write at length. I believe that problem stems from our schools, where students are typically encouraged to write reports that are as long as possible.

What an Executive Summary Should Accomplish ...For You

The executive summary should serve several purposes, both for you and for readers of the business plan. For you, it should accomplish the following:

1. Crystallize your thoughts. Since the executive summary is the business plan in miniature, it contains the plan's highlights, its key points. To write an executive summary, focus on the issues that are most important to your business's success—past and future—and set aside those matters that are tangential.

2. Set priorities. The executive summary, like the business plan, should be organized according to the items' order of importance. Writing it forces you to pick and choose from among the many points you want to make in the business plan and decide on their order of importance.

3. Provide the foundation of the full plan. Once you've written a version of the executive summary, you've made the process of writing the plan much easier. Suddenly, you've provided yourself with a takeoff point for each section of the plan.

55

The four or five sentences that summarize the means of making the product or providing the service give you the basis for that section of the plan. As we all know, it's much easier to begin writing with something on the page than it is to begin with a blank page.

...For Readers

For readers of your business plan, the executive summary is usually the first stop in the reading process. (This assumes that the executive summary is at the very beginning of the plan and that the reader goes from front to back. You can control the former, but not the latter. Some investors, for instance, turn first to the founders' résumés and others to the marketing section.) In any case, from the readers' perspective, your executive summary should have the following attributes:

1. Capture others' attention and imagination. This is particularly important if you want your plan to help you get a bank loan or attract investment funds. But any reader should be intrigued with your executive summary. It intrigues readers most by conveying your commitment to—and excitement about—the business.

2. Make readers want to read more. Because bankers, investors, and financial types have more business plans to read than they have time for, they have to decide easily and quickly which ones to analyze carefully. The executive summary helps them make that decision. Thus, if you hope to obtain financing from the plan, the executive summary has to keep the banker or investor interested. Otherwise, that person will not go further in the plan.

3. Convey the flavor of the rest of the plan. Readers should have a good feeling about your business and what the rest of the plan will cover. The executive summary must succeed in capturing the enthusiasm and energy that resonate through the plan as a whole.

How the Executive Summary Works Its Magic

There's no easy way to tell someone else how to write. People develop their own approaches to writing: the best time of day, whether to type or write longhand, and so forth. An important guideline to keep in mind, especially as you're struggling to write a first draft of an executive summary, is that the key to successful writing is rewriting. Don't expect that first draft to be your final draft or anywhere close to your final draft.

One question to consider is whether the executive summary should be written before the full business plan is written. Certainly you can argue that an executive summary that is true to the full business plan, in fact and in spirit, should be written after the plan is completed. At least it would seem to be easier.

For some entrepreneurs, that might be the correct path to follow. As I've noted, there's no one right way to write a business plan.

I don't agree with that approach, though. I feel you should take a double-barrel approach—write an executive summary before you write the business plan and then rewrite it *after* you complete your plan. My experience is that taking this approach will have a number of benefits:

1. It will help guide your writing of the business plan. You will quickly spots gaps and problems that must be tended to in writing the full plan.

2. It will give you more confidence about the writing that must follow. Once you put a draft of the executive summary down on paper, you will find that the rest of the writing process becomes less intimidating. That's because you will already have written out your thoughts for each area of the plan.

3. It will lead to a better final product. If rewriting is the key to successful writing, then doing versions of the executive summary before and after writing the plan should lead ultimately to a better product. That's because you'll be massaging and reworking the executive summary more times, at different phases.

Keep in mind. . . That initial executive summary will look different to you after you've done the things I suggest in later chapters. Indeed, it may seem almost comical in its inadequacy. Take that as a sign of your progress in mastering the art of putting together a business plan.

Ask Yourself: Would You Invest?

As you begin to write your executive summary, consider not so much what you want to say, but what a prospective investor (or acquirer or key employee) wants to read. That person wants to be convinced that your business is going to be a winner. When you read your executive summary, you must constantly ask yourself: *If someone handed me this executive summary, would I seriously consider investing in this company?*

The best way to write your executive summary draft is to draw on the building blocks suggested in the previous two chapters and to study well-done executive summaries.

• **The building blocks.** Each stage in the planning/writing process, if done right, makes the next stage easier. Based on guidance offered in Chapters 2 and 3, you should already have some written material on which to base the first draft of the executive summary.

In Chapter 2, I advised you to put together an initial table of contents for your business plan, based on the list of subjects that every business plan should cover. I suggested you make notes under each section about the material you expected to cover.

In Chapter 3, I suggested you have the members of your management team write drafts of individual business plan chapters, based on their areas of expertise (assuming you have a management team). While they will need some time to complete this task, you can ask each as a first step to provide initial drafts of summaries of their chapters. From your table of contents and management team summaries, you can write a first draft of the executive summary.

• **Real plans.** By studying examples of other entrepreneurs' executive summaries, both bad and good, you can begin setting your own standards. So I've provided an example of a poorly done executive summary and a well-done executive summary, along with an analysis of the strengths and weaknesses of each.

The Bad Executive Summary: Electronic Parts Inc.

The executive summary in Exhibit 4–1 is actually an altered and disguised version of a real executive summary. But it remains as badly done in this state as it was in its original one. What's wrong with it? You can probably spot some problems, but here are four prominent ones:

1. It says little about the company's strategy. In the contents listed in Chapter 2, information about the company and its strategy was near the top of the list. How does the company plan to carry out its goals, and what evidence can it offer that it will succeed?

2. It barely touches on marketing issues. We learn that the company's product serves an industry with "excessive industrial demands," but there's little explanation or corroboration. What is meant by excessive, in quantitative terms, and how will the company take advantage of the situation?

3. It focuses too heavily on the company's financial needs. Obviously, this business plan is intended as a financing document, but the company's financial needs are overemphasized. Yet there's nothing about the company's financial projections.

Investors want to know how management will make the investment grow and pay them back with a hefty return.

4. It is internally directed rather than externally directed. Readers learn about the company's plans for building a plant and hiring people, along with the founder's qualifications. But they learn little about where these efforts will take the company in the marketplace.

Of course, you will likely see other weaknesses, such as the lack of explanation about the competition and the management team. But essentially, the business plan's authors wasted space; by devoting so much time to certain issues, they neglected others. It's hard to get excited about the business plan.

A Better Executive Summary: People Express

In one page, the People Express executive summary (Exhibit 4–2) gives us a clear sense of why this company will succeed. The executive summary accomplishes its mission by doing the following:

1. Explains why the timing is right. The need for frequent jet commuter service between major cities of the Northeast, along with deregulation to encourage lower airfares, are the principal reasons for starting a new airline. We learn that in the first few sentences.

2. Establishes its strategy. People Express will use experienced managers to market the company more aggressively and hire smarter than others in the industry. In other words, the new company will be able to respond more quickly to marketplace changes than the well-established and entrenched companies that constituted the airline industry at that time.

3. Explains how it will compete effectively. We learn in the executive summary that People Express won't have to deal with a unionized work force and will achieve economies of scale that reduce cost-per-seat mile by 30% to 40% from then-existing airlines.

4. It is terse and to the point. There's no waste of space or words. The points are made in bulleted form, one after another. There's no time for the eyes to glaze over.

The timetable summary complements the executive summary. It provides a quick reference for the company's short-term plans.

Still, even this executive summary has flaws. It neglects to project the company's revenues over the first three to five years. Nor does it state how much financing is required. And while it alludes to the company's experienced management, it doesn't provide enough details about their impressive qualifications.

Clearly, the pros don't always do it exactly right either.

EXERCISES

Worksheets for this chapter are provided on page 212

The following four executive summaries are composites based on real executive summaries. Read each carefully, and then answer the following questions:

1. Which two are the most effective executive summaries?

2. Which two are the least effective executive summaries?

3. In the best executive summaries, describe the three most important strengths.

4. In the worst executive summaries, list the three most significant weaknesses.

5. What would you do to strengthen the worst ones?

EXERCISE 4-A:
EXECUTIVE SUMMARY:
RODNEY FOSTER ASSOCIATES

Rodney Foster Associates is a highly qualified group of public relations executives based in Indianapolis, Indiana. The president is Mr. Foster, who is highly experienced, first as a business reporter with the Associated Press and then as chief of public relations for PepsiCoke. All five of the firm's top representatives have experience at *Fortune* 500 companies in either public relations or corporate communications.

At Rodney Foster Associates we pride ourselves on our ability to write clearly and design attractive media kits. This combination of skills enables us to produce excellent public relations materials that make our clients look their best to the outside world.

We expect our growing reputation to lead to the new clients necessary to support our anticipated growth. As clients see the attractive news releases and media kits that we produce, we are certain that word about our skills will spread, leading to new contracts via referrals. This approach will allow Rodney Foster Associates to concentrate on producing the best-quality media materials, without being diverted by the need to spend time and resources on marketing and sales.

In our first three years we have received seven small contracts, but we expect that as our reputation spreads, our work load will increase. When this occurs, we will need additional well-qualified public relations representatives.

In addition, our skills are expanding. We are preparing to organize seminars for clients and train them for television appearances. We expect Rodney Foster Associates to become a full-service public relations firm, capable of taking on any assignment. We will work with any type of client, preferring not to limit ourselves to any one industry or type of company.

As our public relations reputation and skills expand, we expect to add four more PR professionals to the six we now have and two administrative assistants to the three we now have, all within the next four years.

Rodney Foster Associates has operated at near break-even during its first three years. But we expect the local corporate world to seek out our services and enable us to achieve our growth objectives over the next four years.

EXHIBIT 4-B:

EXECUTIVE SUMMARY:
THE KANSAS CITY ARCHITECTURAL GROUP

The Kansas City Architectural Group is a nine-person firm that includes six well-trained and experienced architects supported by two drafters and an administrative assistant. Gross revenues have averaged $550,000 annually, mainly in medical office design, over the past three years. During the last year, sales began to increase.

The firm's goal is to pass the $1-million revenue mark within three years and the $1.3-million mark in five years. We will require 14 people to handle the $1-million sales.

The Kansas City Architectural Group expects to achieve its revenue goals through an aggressive marketing program that includes:

- Direct contacts provided by existing clients and networking;
- Regularly planned publication of newspaper and magazine articles describing its work and its viewpoints;
- Seminars for existing and prospective clients on new architectural approaches for improving the operations of systems in aging facilities.
- An expanded public relations effort that includes news releases announcing contracts received and human interest stories about our personnel.

All employees consider themselves an important part of the firm's marketing effort. This attitude and approach has enabled the firm to grow to its present size in only three years and is expected to lead to a near doubling in size over the next three years.

By concentrating on designing medical facilities, the Kansas City Architectural Group doesn't allow itself to be distracted from what it does best. The firm intends to continue in the area of medical facilities, in an effort to undertake larger projects.

The firm encourages its staff members to improve their professional skills by sending them to professional meetings and contributing to the cost of additional education. Because of its efforts to recognize and stimulate employee growth, the Kansas City Architectural Group has had minimal employee turnover. Its employees truly are and will remain its most important asset as the firm continues its rapid growth.

The firm now has a $200,000 revolving line of credit with the First National Bank of Kansas City. It seeks to increase that by $100,000 in each of the next three years, in line with expected revenue growth.

EXERCISE 4-C:

EXECUTIVE SUMMARY:
THE GREEN THUMB

The Green Thumb is a highly successful garden center that is rapidly outgrowing its existing Chicago facilities. The company plans to renovate and expand its facilities to increase per-customer sales to existing customers and to attract more new upscale customers.

Such expansion and renovation will enable the company to achieve sales over the next three years of $3.1 million and over the next five years of $4 million from expected 1986 sales of $1.8 million. Moreover, pretax profit margins are expected to increase to between 17% and 22% from the current 5%.

The renovation and expansion will enable the company to capitalize further on its premier location on Broadway on the North Side serving an urban market not extremely knowledgeable about horticultural products and thus open to sales upgrades. The facilities improvement will also enable the company to build sales during traditionally slow periods and fill in the gaps between the three existing peaks of spring, fall, and Christmas.

The company also seeks to reduce high work force turnover brought on by the seasonal sales fluctuations. The Green Thumb in its improved facilities will be able to capitalize on its more even sales by retaining a highly trained work force. This work force can use its knowledge about horticultural products to improve sales effectiveness.

Similarly, the company seeks to sell high-priced, high-margin containers, lawn furniture, and gift items it doesn't have space to stock in its existing facilities; such items are necessary to substantially increase revenues and profits. The new facilities will enable management to take advantage of its superior knowledge of the intricate supply-side in horticultural products to expand its product line. The company has already taken steps to guarantee an increase in low-cost annual and perennial supplies by leasing 43 acres of land in Palos Heights.

The company has built an experienced and expert management team to work with its founder and chief executive officer, Bradley Turner, to take maximum advantage of the expanded facilities. Moreover, the company plans to provide intense training and equity incentives to upgrade its entire staff and motivate it to aspire to management positions.

The Green Thumb seeks a $500,000 bank loan to finance the facilities upgrading. The renovation and expansion will involve three phases to be completed over a year. Substantial revenue growth should become apparent within two years. The company seeks an agreement that will provide for loan repayment over eight years.

4

The Executive
Summary as a
Guiding Light

EXERCISE 4-D:

Executive Summary:
Cherry Tree Technologies

Cherry Tree Technologies publishes ONLINE, a widely recognized disk monthly for Compaq computers. Periodical disk publishing is in its infancy, and Cherry Tree Technologies has the opportunity to become a market leader for all PC disk publications. ONLINE has proved the viability and potential profitability of its magazine on a disk or disk monthly concept and has expanded its success on Compaq computers.

Some of the primary benefits to subscribers of ONLINE are:

1. Variety of Programs
2. Entertainment Value
3. Overall Usefulness
4. Low Cost
5. Ease of Use

The ONLINE publications by Cherry Tree Technologies are the primary source of revenue for the company at this time. However, there are additional software sales through ONLINE's catalog of products to which it has the rights and a small amount of sales of software from other vendors. The company plans to expand its software sales area as it grows to provide more complete services to the PC aftermarket subscriber base.

The ONLINE Disk Monthly is not a concept unique to Cherry Tree, but the success it has achieved in recent months is unparalleled. The competition to date in this field has been weak or unsuccessful, and ONLINE currently has the opportunity to capture the leadership position for all disk publications.

The company, founded in 1989, spent 1990 determining the best path for success and can now concentrate on a dramatic growth opportunity currently available to it. Through the first eight months of 1991, the company achieved $350,000 sales; for the rest of this year the company expects $600,000 revenue. Next year the company projects $4 million revenue, with $6 million in 1993, $10 million in 1994, and $20 million in 1995.

These projections are based on proven formulas for success in marketing the ONLINE for Compaq so far. The formula was developed by the new management teams, which reorganized the company in February/March. Projections have been exceeded in every month since March. The company is thus a new business situation with an unusual growth opportunity over the next five years.

EXHIBIT 4-1:

EXECUTIVE SUMMARY:
ELECTRONIC COMPONENTS INC.

Electronic Components Inc. is a start-up company that will make a variety of electronic components, beginning with a new type of aluminum-based capacitor. This unique product, coupled with excessive commercial demand for capacitor devices, will provide us with an ample share of the capacitor market and numerous opportunities for expansion into related electronic components.

The founders are dedicated and determined to make the venture a successful and profitable entity. Technical expertise is provided by James F. Lynch, who has been involved in designing capacitors for 11 years. He obtained a Bachelor of Science degree in electronic engineering from the Massachusetts Institute of Technology.

Technology for capacitors is changing rapidly. Electronic Components Inc. has an opportunity to capitalize on a major technological change by getting off to a quick start and expanding quickly.

This proposal pertains to two additional phases of required financing. The first phase, consisting of about $150,000 for pilot plant start-up, has been completed from the personal funds of the principals. The remaining financing is for the following:

Phase Two: Obtain $750,000 capital for:
- Hiring and training production personnel;
- Purchasing additional equipment necessary for appropriate productivity;
- Develop the market;
- Complete the sales rep network;
- Explore new markets.

Phase Three: Increase production and sales
- Computerize manufacturing to triple output with minimal increase in labor;
- Begin exporting;
- Expand new marketing activity.

Financing will be used to purchase manufacturing equipment, hire the necessary employees, and develop new markets. In addition, management intends to spend between 10% and 20% of revenues on research and development of new products.

The electronics component field offers attractive opportunities for fast sales and profit growth. Already, demand exceeds supply in the capacitor area as well as in other related areas.

EXHIBIT 4-2:

EXECUTIVE SUMMARY:
PEOPLE EXPRESS

The Eastern seaboard of the United States is ripe for the entry of a new, superefficient, low-cost air carrier to provide quick, reliable inter-city air transportation. Such an entity would bring to the Northeast the same benefits that have accrued to other areas of the United States. Chief among these are:

- Frequent jet commuter service between major cities
- Prices competitive with private automobiles
- Fulfillment of congressional goals in enacting the Airline Deregulation Act of 1978 to have better service at lower fares

The new company will be able to achieve these goals for the following reasons:

- Aggressive, innovative management that has been tested in the field and been on the leading edge of innovation in air transportation marketing and systems
- Equipment and facilities designed specifically for the low-cost production of air transportation
- Manpower selected, trained, and motivated to be efficient and profit oriented
- New systems to be applied to the entire business of air transportation to minimize investment in manpower and machines

All of these, when applied to the new entity, will result in considerable economies vis-à-vis exisiting air carriers.

- 40 years of regulation have created an industry heavily unionized with tremendous inefficiencies
- The economics of a new entity should be at least 30%–40% better per seat mile that the current trunks
- Other new carriers such as Southwest or Air Florida have shown a consistent ability to compete on a price basis and earn extraordinary returns
- The current political, economic, and regulatory climate is ideal for the proposal herein envisioned
- The Northeast is waiting for someone to bring it what the rest of the nation already has: low airfares.

PRELIMINARY TIMETABLE

March 1, 1980	Obtain initial financing
April 1, 1980	Hire core group to do work on air carrier systems and procedures
May 1, 1980	File with Civil Aeronautics Board for certificate
Fall, 1980	Second round of financing completed
October 1, 1980	Receive Certificate of Public Convenience and Necessity from Civil Aeronautics Board
November 1, 1980	Begin public awareness campaign on new airline, goals and objectives
	Secure facilities/offices etc. needed for 6/1/81 start date
January 1, 1981	Begin selection process for key employees
	Finalize equipment program for first 10 planes
February 1, 1981	Apply to FAA for approval to operate
	Negotiate with others for support contracts
April 1, 1981	Finalize operating plans for publication
May 1, 1981	Receive FAA approval to operate
June 1, 1981	Commence revenue operations

PART TWO:

ANSWERING
THE KEY BUSINESS
QUESTIONS

Company Strategy: What's Your Identity?

EVERY COMPANY is driven by an underlying philosophy and logic. These may never have been articulated by the founders, either verbally or in writing. But they are there, whether the owners and employees realize it. The philosophy and logic may be expressed in your efforts to decentralize decision making in the company. They may be expressed in your decision to finance the company entirely from earnings rather than seek outside money. The section on the company is where you spell out your company's philosophy and logic—its reason for being, its identity. This section of the business plan should cover four principal issues:

1. Company strategy. "Strategy" is a fancy term for your company's overall approach to producing and selling its products and/or services—and its goals for maximizing success. You should have some guiding principles to the way you operate that allow you to succeed and that distinguish you from the competition.

2. Mission statement. Increasing numbers of executives are concluding that, in addition to an overall strategy, they should develop some kind of statement that encapsulates their companies' values and overall purpose in life. The mission statement, when articulated and used effectively, can unify a company's employees.

3. Technology/information assessment. For more and more companies, technology and information management have become central to overall success—influencing such matters as production schedules, order-turnaround times, and financial integrity. Investors, bankers, and other financial types are coming around to the view that a company's ability to use technology and manage information is a key determinant of success in today's fast-changing world; therefore, a vital part of a company's strategy and identity should include an assessment of the role of technology and information in the company's growth.

4. Management team. Who determines and implements strategy? The people who guide the company must have credibility, based on their accomplishments with other organizations or with the current company.

This all sounds straightforward, except for one important proviso: it all has to fit together into a coherent whole. The strategy has to be consistent and realistic.

It's very difficult to write a business plan that sells your business effectively if the strategy, mission, technology, and management team are not compatible. Take the case of a 14-year-old company that produces special types of bearings for the aerospace industry. The company is headed by its original founder, an electrical engineer in his early fifties, who was educated at the Massachusetts Institute of Technology. His "team" consists of a half-dozen junior engineers who graduated from colleges little known outside of their communities in the Northeast.

During its 14-year history, the company had recorded

annual sales ranging from $350,000 to $800,000, with no consistent upward or downward trend. For the past three years, though, the company has been losing new orders to competitors because the design of its bearings had fallen behind technologically.

The founder put together a business plan seeking to raise $1.5 million of financing, based on his strategy—as described in the company section of the business plan—of upgrading the product's technology and assembling an experienced management team with the goal of achieving 25% sales growth over each of the coming five years. That was all well and good, except for a few problems:

- How could a company that had shown inconsistent sales growth over the previous 14 years be expected to suddenly achieve consistently rising sales for the next 5 years?

- How could a founder and chief executive who had failed to assemble a real management team be expected suddenly to change and recruit executives who were at his level in their training and experience?

- How could any shareholder be sure that the chief executive who had let his company fall behind in its industry's technology wouldn't allow the same thing to happen again?

In other words, the strategy, technology, and team this CEO planned just didn't mesh with what had gone on before. Moreover, he didn't have a mission. Needless to say, he didn't raise the money he was seeking. Had he recruited a CEO with a track record of success in assembling a management team and growing a business, the results might have been different.

The remainder of this chapter provides guidance for writing the company section of the business plan so that it creates a logical and consistent identity for the company.

**The Strategy:
Playing Historian
and Futurist**

As I've noted, a company's strategy is a statement of its overall approach to doing business, its goals, and how it plans to achieve those goals. In the context of the business plan, the strategy can usually be summarized in a few sentences that articulate the company's expectations for growth in coming years and the steps that will be required to make it happen.

Software Publishing Corp. stated its strategy this way: "Software Publishing Corp. is positioning itself as the leading independent software supplier for personal computers by producing products aimed at the fastest-growing segment of the personal computer market: Business/Professional applications. SPC's unique strength in this segment is its ability to produce software that turns the personal computer into a versatile problem-solving tool that individuals can use to describe and solve a problem in their own unique way without programming."

A distributor of pharmaceutical supplies that had grown from $5 million to $25 million in annual sales over eight years wanted to continue its growth, but had to overcome some problems. Chief among these were profits under 5% of sales, excessive employee turnover, and difficulties managing inventory well enough to keep stores stocked in a timely way. So it stated its strategy this way:

THE COMPANY'S MAIN OBJECTIVES ARE:
1. Achieve annual sales of $50 million annually in five years, with after-tax net profit of 12%;
2. Deliver 95% or more of its customer orders when promised or earlier;
3. Reduce employee turnover from 40% annually to 15% in two years and to less than 10% in three years.

While this statement sets lofty goals, the written analysis must also provide sufficient information to make the strategy *believable*. One effective approach is to break the section on strategy down into three parts—past, present, and future.

1. History. Here—usually under the title "Background"—you explain the company's origin and development. When was it founded and what was its original strategy? How has the company progressed and how has its strategy changed? Why did the strategy change? Perhaps trends changed. Some restaurant chains that originally emphasized steak and other beef products, for example, discovered that the public's increasing preference for chicken and fish over beef meant that they had to alter their strategies appropriately.

The history should include facts and figures about such fundamentals as sales, profits, number of employees, and locations. Of course, successes should be emphasized. But if there were problems that led to sales declines and/or losses, along with changes in strategy, these should be acknowledged and explained. A rapidly growing maker of burglar alarms and other security systems, for instance, encountered two level sales years when it sued a competitor for suspected infringement on a patent. The company's officials explained in the history that the suit preoccupied management and drained badly needed resources from the growth effort. Outside investors and others evaluating the company would probably consider this an extenuating circumstance.

2. Current status. This section provides a snapshot of the company today. What are its strengths and weaknesses?

Most business owners are quick to extol their company's strengths—the high quality of its product and/or service, its acceptance in the marketplace, the loyalty of the employees, and so forth. Not surprisingly, weaknesses rarely get much attention. And why should they? Most entrepreneurs don't see many weaknesses in their businesses and, if they do, they'd prefer not to put them in writing. Especially if bankers, prospective executives, and others will be reading the plan.

But as I pointed out in Chapter 3, weaknesses should be faced squarely. For one thing, everyone who will read your plan is perfectly aware that all companies have weaknesses. For another, your willingness to acknowledge and describe those weaknesses helps portray you as an open-minded, honest, and smart manager. Finally, you may find that dealing openly with problems actually helps your business plan better achieve its goals.

A clothing retailer had grown so much that it needed to add a new facility—and obtain a bank loan to pay for the expansion. The business plan pointed out, "Demand for the company's products is now so strong that the business has become facilities-limited. On weekends, in particular, lines of customers at the cashier's station discourage other customers eager to make purchases and result in lost sales."

Thus, the company defines a serious problem as an opportunity—one that a bank can help exploit by lending the company $1 million.

3. Future prospects. This section, usually titled "Objectives," is where entrepreneurs can sometimes get carried away. Being the optimists that they are, entrepreneurs are invariably projecting all kinds of wonderful things, most of which revolve around all the money their companies will make.

It's easy to project sales and earnings rising at 15% to 20% annually for each of the next five years. It's harder to make those projections believable. If the company has a history of growth or is showing signs of markedly improving results, then the predictions for the future become more believable. An outside trend can help make the predictions more believable. For instance, many companies providing medical equipment and services are basing their growth projections on demographic trends that show America's population growing older.

What if the company is a start-up and has no history or current operating situation from which to extrapolate trends? In one sense, the start-up has more freedom than existing companies to make projections. There's no experience to dispel the optimism. But there is one factor that can make the projections of a start-up more or less believable, and that is the composition and quality of the management team.

If the people starting a company have a history of success, their optimism becomes more plausible, as I will discuss in the section that follows.

Keep in mind. . . "Strategy" is one of those business terms that is often bandied about quite loosely. Don't get bogged down in terminology. The key issue is explaining your company's overall approach for achieving growth and profits.

The Mission Statement: A Big-Picture View

If a company's strategy represents its overall approach to maximizing business success—stated in terms of achieving certain sales, profits, product delivery, and employee turnover goals—then the mission statement represents a more generalized and idealistic vision of the company's purpose in life. If done right, a mission statement can go a long way toward energizing everyone in an organization to achieve the ideal.

Unfortunately, in the rush to develop mission statements, many companies have established statements that are somehow too general and lofty. I have seen a number of mission statements that commit companies to being "the producer of the highest-quality (name the product) in the world" or "the top company in the (name the industry)."

In my experience, the best mission statements are oriented in either of two directions:

1. They help people improve their lives. Most employees want to believe that their jobs or professions are somehow doing something beyond simply making money. Yes, there is much satisfaction to be achieved by being successful financially, but if that success can be combined with making a contribution to society's betterment, the company has achieved a powerful motivational tool.

The CML Group, a small conglomerate of leisure products companies that includes the Carroll Reed women's clothing retail chain and NordicTrack exercise equipment, has as its mission, "To create products that enhance people's

- Health;
- Understanding of the natural world;
- Sense of well-being."

According to Charles Leighton, the company's chief executive, "We wanted something that excites our young people beyond just saying, 'We'll increase sales X percent a year.'"

CML Group has been extremely successful, achieving a compound growth rate for sales in excess of 20% annually since its founding in 1973.

2. They establish achievable goals. Mission statements can become the basis of rallying points that excite employees and in the end excite customers. One of the most successful companies in this regard is Ben & Jerry's. Its founders decided that in order to avoid the overly general mission statement, they would develop three different sets of missions:

- A product mission that essentially commits the company to making a top-quality innovative product.
- An economic mission that commits the executives to running the company in a prudent and caring way in order to be profitable and provide an ongoing source of jobs.
- A social mission focused on serving the community, which comprises the company's customer base.

It is the last mission that has most galvanized employees. Based on that mission, the company decided that children are the basis of its social mission. Thus, it organized a campaign in the early 1990s to help abused children, under the motto, "Leave no child behind." Working jointly with the Washington-based Children's Defense Fund, Ben & Jerry's organized entertainment festivals around the country, complete with free ice cream, at which attendees were asked to purchase postcards for

25¢ apiece to write their congressional representatives to take action toward reducing child abuse.

The festivals generated a torrent of mail to Washington and no doubt sensitized senators and representatives about the importance of protecting children from abuse. Not coincidentally, the festivals enabled consumers to sample the company's ice cream as well as to associate the company with a worthy cause.

A note of caution. . . For the mission statement to achieve its goal of galvanizing employees, it should be developed with as much input from employees as possible. Developing an effective mission statement isn't an easy or simple process. It will likely create a good deal of discussion and debate about what is appropriate, achievable, and useful for the company to establish as its mission. Such discussion and debate are useful because they invariably raise worthwhile issues about the company's purpose. Probably the worst approach is for the chief executive to devise a mission statement and then force it on the rest of the management team and employees.

Technology/ Information Assessment

If there is one single factor that has enabled small growing companies to compete on a level playing field with large corporations it is the availability of ever greater computer and other technological capacity at lower costs. Entrepreneurs can now easily acquire the computer power that during the 1960s and 1970s filled entire rooms of large corporations and cost many hundreds of thousands of dollars.

Increasingly, technology and information management are being used by small growing companies to achieve competitive advantages. Mail-order firms can immediately access past buying records of customers who call in orders, determine availability of products, make the charges, and initiate the packing and shipping—all with a few keystroke taps on the computer.

Small manufacturers and distributors can give overseas distributors access to computer networks that allow viewing of backlogs, inventories, and other essential information.

The effect of such advances is to allow companies with the appropriate technologies to service their customers more quickly and efficiently than competitors lacking the technology. Thus, a dry cleaner that can access the records of a customer by entering the last four digits of his or her phone number has an advantage over a dry cleaner that must manually search through all the clothing on its racks for a customer who has lost a cleaning slip.

In discussing their approach to doing business, companies should articulate how technology and information management fit into the operations and ongoing success of their companies. This is about more than how the accounting or database management takes place. I'm talking here about the integration of technology into the company's most important operations—an overall business system of technology and information management.

The Management Team

The quality of the people running the company is a critical link in making the strategy believable. Clearly, if there's a history of company accomplishment and growth, that speaks for itself. For a company seeking to convince outsiders of its ability to succeed in the future, the quality of the management team becomes extremely important. Many investors and other outsiders are known to turn first to the descriptions of the management team when reading a business plan. They know that the people are key to determining success, and they are looking for clues to tell them that the people have what it takes to guide the company through growth stages.

The two most common management team problems are best described as follows:

1. The "one-man band" syndrome. I should point out that a company that expects to be a slow-growing lifestyle business should view the one-man band approach to business operations as merely a syndrome. It becomes a problem only if the company plans to expand significantly. In too many growth-oriented businesses, a single entrepreneur controls the company, makes the decisions, and is the guiding force for expansion. But beyond a certain point, usually about $1 million of sales, it becomes impossible for one person to control everything. A key concern of bankers and investors is who else will be involved in executive decision making.

2. Everyone comes from the same background. People tend to be friends with those with whom they have a lot in common. That's fine for friendships, but it's less fine for management teams. When everyone in a high-tech company is an engineer or everyone in an interior design firm is a designer, it means there aren't any financial or marketing or sales experts. Successful management teams require diversity of training and expertise.

In describing the management team in the business plan, I offer the following suggestions:

• *Emphasize real-life business accomplishments.* To get clues about an individual's likelihood for future success, you must know what that person has done in the past. In a start-up, ideally management team members will have helped run or begun a previous company that was at least moderately successful. Or they will have managed a division of a large company that showed impressive growth and accomplishment. Failing those accomplishments, outstanding job performance should be emphasized, especially if it demonstrates sound business judgment. Educational credentials are less important unless the business is technology oriented and some of the key officials are academics whose research accomplishments are essential to the company's product development.

For an existing business, previous performance becomes the

83

key measurement criterion. The point is that an individual is more likely to manage a business successfully in the future if he or she has done so in the past.

• *Identify evidence of special knowledge and creativity.* Increasingly, business success is determined by top management's leading-edge skills and the ability to apply those skills in unorthodox ways. For example, the management team at a computer software firm defied the conventional wisdom in its industry by launching a massive give-away campaign of a $50 personal finance program. The campaign attracted wide media attention. More significantly for the company, it added a million names to the company's user list, enabling it to sell upgrades and other products to a friendly audience. The business plan should mention any evidence of unusual knowledge and application of that knowledge.

• *Make the most of your resources.* Be sure to mention and describe everyone in a position of authority and responsibility. It's easy to overlook individuals who have managerial duties without having fancy titles. You may even want to change some titles to emphasize the individuals' importance. (The sales director may become your vice-president of marketing.) The point is, if you're seeking outside support, you want to portray a real team.

• *Describe your board of directors.* This assumes you have a board that includes outsiders as well as the inside executives. A board of experienced executives, industry experts, and other credible individuals demonstrates an additional strength.

• *Keep it brief.* A paragraph or two on each of the key people and their major business accomplishments is all that is necessary. Include résumés at the end of the business plan, in an appendix.

Describing Strategy: The Pizza Hut Model

In its 1976 business plan, Pizza Hut provides an excellent model for the section on the company. Pizza Hut's descriptions of the company are distributed through several chapters, but essentially the company uses the three parts—history, current status, and objectives—described earlier in this chapter. Exhibits 5–1 through 5–3 reproduce excerpts that demonstrate the Pizza Hut approach.

Because Pizza Hut was 18 years old when this business plan was written, there was a long history to cover. Under the chapter title, "How Did We Get Where We Are Today?" the plan's authors gave a year-by-year chronology of the company's history, beginning with its founding in 1958. While this section is six pages long, the first three pages reproduced here (see Exhibit 5–1) convey the flavor of what's included.

Note that the writing is straightforward and not self-congratulatory. Indeed, the second page points out difficulties the company faced in a 1969 expansion effort and blames "total organization impulsiveness" for the problems.

The 11-page chapter on the company's current status is entitled, "Our Business Is." It is divided into sections on operations, domestic franchises, international operations, and various non–Pizza Hut restaurants and ventures.

In this chapter, we learn about the number of outlets, the breakdown of franchised versus company-owned outlets, the type of products sold, and new products being tested. The first four pages of the chapter reproduced here (see Exhibit 5–2) give the reader a good idea of how the company is doing and what executives feel make it successful.

As for the future, we get a one-page summary of objectives under the title, "Corporate Strategy." As you can see in Exhibit 5–3, it consists of a list of priorities that include improving sales and profits, positioning the company for financing, exploiting new markets, modernizing outlets, and so forth. The objectives are general, as the section notes, "to allow specific supporting plans to be developed."

CHAPTER FIVE

EXERCISES

Worksheets for this chapter are provided on page 214

1. Describe your company's strategy as briefly as possible—in a maximum of five sentences.

2. Define your company's mission in three sentences or less.

3. Explain realistically, in a few paragraphs, how your company's management team will achieve its strategy.

4. Explain in a few paragraphs how your company plans to use technology and manage information to improve the likelihood of overall success.

5. If a conflict exists between your company's strategy, mission, and technology plans and its past accomplishments, how will you deal with the inconsistency?

EXHIBIT 5-1:

PIZZA HUT:
COMPANY HISTORY

FROM THE BUSINESS PLAN OF PIZZA HUT

HOW DID WE GET WHERE WE ARE TODAY?

Calendar
Year

1958   Wichita, Kansas, became the home of the first Pizza Hut restaurant when Daniel M. Carney, Frank L. Carney, and John W. Bender opened their first unit at 503 South Bluff.

1959   Pizza Hut, Inc. was incorporated in the state of Kansas and the first franchise unit was opened in Topeka, Kansas, by Dick Hassur.

1962   PHI bought out John Bender's interest and Robert Chisholm joined the company as treasurer.

1963   PHI was recognized as a viable concept for further expansion and the uniform freestanding design for Pizza Hut units was adopted.

1967   The International Pizza Hut Franchise Holders Association (IPHFHA) was organized.

1968   In its reorganization, PHI acquired the capital stock of 129 franchised corporations that had been operating 122 units. The company's first move into the international arena came with the opening of a unit in Canada.

1969   • On January 30, after meeting the requirements of the Securities Exchange Commission (SEC), PHI offered 410,000 shares of its common stock to the public.
        • PHI acquired three additional restaurant divisions—Taco Kid, Next Door, and the Flaming Steer—two supply companies, Franchise Services, Inc. (an equipment company), and J&C Food Co., Inc. (a food and supply distributor).

- Two new departments were established—R&D (Research & Development) and MIS (Management Information Services) and the Real Estate department was centralized in Wichita.
- The Qualified Stock Option Plan was adopted by PHI.
- The administrative problems of inadequacy in planning led to organization impulsiveness in making expansion-related decisions and in operational control.
- First major revisions were made to the Operations Manual in keeping with the changes in the company.
- PHI achieved the status of "first" in number of pizza units.

1970
- PHI was reincorporated in the state of Delaware.
- A new international headquarters building was opened in Wichita and the company moved further into the international market by opening units in Munich, Germany, and Sydney, Australia.
- PHI acquired 80% of Ready Italy (a frozen crust manufacturing company) and formed Sunflower Food Processors, Inc. as a joint venture with Sunflower Beef, Inc.
- The Field Reporting System (FRS) became an effective control system for Pizza Hut units.
- The Pizza Hut Operations Regional Managers were centralized in Wichita, and the Field Training School was established in the home office. Additionally, the balance sheet cleanup program and the unit management training program (Audiscan) were established.
- PHI recognized its acquisition problems as well as the predictability of the individual Pizza Hut unit.

1971
- PHI established the Management (Planning) Committee, the Franchisee Advisory Board, the Middle Management and Professional Management

programs, the cash management system, and the Corporate Information Department.

• A turnaround was achieved in the Taco Kid operations and PHI became "number one" in pizza sales.

1972   On November 30, PHI was listed on the New York Stock Exchange under the symbol PIZ.

• PHI opened unit number 1,000 and achieved a $1,000,000 sales week in domestic company-owned Pizza Hut restaurants.

• Financing was secured through a public offering (WhiteWeld) and long-term debt financing agreements were made.

• The Phase III training program and three new departments—Marketing, Human Resources, and Public Programs—were established and the first Pizza Hut Basketball Classic was held in Las Vegas, Nevada.

• A second distribution center was added in Peoria, Illinois, PHI's joint venture in Japan was finalized, and the first foreign acquisitions were made in Canada and Mexico.

• General Resources Corporation went public and changed its name to Pizza Corporation of America.

• PHI increased the number of its officers and added two outside members to the Board of Directors.

• The first five-year corporate plan was published.

1973   • The 35x65 Pizza Hut restaurant building was accepted as the standard company building.

• PHI sold the Flaming Steer, Next Door, and Ready Italy operations, and Sunflower Food Products was acquired by FSI. Taco Kid units were converted to Fiesta Cantina restaurants.

EXHIBIT 5-2:

PIZZA HUT:
THE CURRENT STATUS OF THE COMPANY

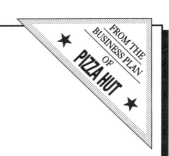

OUR BUSINESS IS

Our customers define our business! The following relates to what our customers have told us over the years—and how we have changed to meet their needs, wants, and desires. The more our people know about our business, the more they will contribute toward its progress.

PHI is the largest chain of pizza restaurants in both number of units and sales.

PHI is principally engaged in the operation, development, franchising, and servicing of a system of restaurants under the name "Pizza Hut." Pizza Hut restaurants feature pizza, pasta products, sandwiches, beverages, and a limited menu of complementary food products at moderate prices prepared under recipes and procedures developed and/or prescribed by PHI, and they are constructed in accordance with a distinctive exterior and interior building design.

PHI also manufactures certain fixtures and supplies, processes some pizza ingredients, and distributes equipment, supplies, and food products for use in its restaurants and sale to franchisees.

In addition, PHI operates a limited number of Mexican food restaurants and in December 1974 opened its first test unit of a second concept called Applegate's Landing. Although this concept also features pizza and a limited menu of complementary food products, the menu items are different from those sold in the Pizza Hut restaurants.

The sales growth of the company during the last five years has exceeded 30% per year.

DOMESTIC PIZZA HUT OPERATIONS

Domestic Pizza Hut restaurants, located in 47 states, primarily feature two styles of pizza: Thin 'n Crispy and Thick 'n Chewy—both available with a variety of topping combinations. Additionally, the units offer sandwiches, salads, baked pasta products, and beverages (including beer in most locations). The Company has followed the policy of requiring each Pizza Hut restaurant, whether operated by the company or by our franchisees, to be constructed and operated so that they are similar in exterior appearance and interior decoration, menu, and service. Substantially all of the units are freestanding buildings constructed in a distinctive one-story brick design of approximately 1,500 to 2,600 square feet, including kitchen and storage facilities, seating from 60 to 120 customers. Where certain market conditions exist, exceptions to the basic building design are allowed.

Below is the status of the Domestic Pizza Division as of February 1, 1976:

Co-owned units	Open	Under const.	Lease/ purch.	% Profitable	Ticket average
	1,152(A)	70	72	92.7 (B)	$5.15

(A) Total number of international, franchised, and company-owned stores approximately 2,500.
(B) Profitable at 6,499 on stores open at least six months.

During the first nine months of fiscal 1976, Pizza Hut units experienced average monthly sales growth rates compared to last year of 10.4%.

On a quarter-by-quarter basis, the growth rate of average unit volume was 11.8% for the first quarter, 8.9% for the second quarter, and 10.7% for the third quarter. Stores open one year or more which have had the benefit of the normal maturity process had average unit sales increases of 11.6% for the nine-month period. Total price increases, including an overall 5.25% increase taken basically in November 1975, were 6.1% for the first nine-month period, thereby indicating a real growth of 5.5%.

Each of the company-operated units is the responsibility of a unit manager who is totally accountable for the people, sales, and profits of the unit. The supervision of the individual company units is the responsibility of our Area General Managers, each having approximately six or seven units to supervise. The AGMs, in turn, report directly to a District Manager, who in turn reports to one of nine Regional Managers. On average, each DM has five AGMs reporting to him. In certain isolated cases, an AGM may report directly to one of the RMs. Area General Managers are also responsible for inspecting certain franchise operations and reporting the results of their inspections to the Franchise Department.

Consumer advertising and sales promotion for Pizza Hut restaurants and Pizza Hut products is accomplished by a combination of national and local programs.

With the establishment of the Ad Committee, planning for national advertising, research, and production was shifted to a year which coincides with the Company's fiscal year. It is estimated that $6,000,000 will be spent on national advertising, research, production, and related expenses in fiscal 1977 through contributions of $2.7 million from franchisee-owned units and $3.3 million from company-owned units. This compares to estimated expenditures for fiscal year 1976 of $5 million.

The FY '77 National Schedule will provide a minimum of 29 weeks of network advertising with 2–3 week hiatus periods between flights and 40% more weight (GRP's) per flight than FY '76.

Local advertising and promotion programs are conducted separately from the national program. The Ad Committee provides the bulk of the advertising materials for use in television, radio, and newspapers. These materials are flexible for local adaptation while providing advertising theme consistency with Network Television Advertising.

Currently the majority of local media advertising efforts are planned, scheduled, and conducted in "ADI" (Area of Dominant Influence) programs. The "ADI" program started in January 1973 with thirteen functioning market groups. Today there are 104 functioning "ADIs" covering 65% of total system units.

The purpose of a local program is to coordinate the advertising and promotion efforts so that dollar resources are pooled and concentrated on common goals during a particular promotion period to "promote" one product (Cavatini, Pizza, etc.), one revenue period (lunch, early week dinner, etc.), traffic building offers (specials, premiums, discounts, etc.), and special events (new product introductions, new store openings, Basketball Classic, etc.).

Local advertising expenditures for the company were approximately $942,000, $1,643,000, $1,766,000, and $3,170,800 for fiscal years 1972, 1973, 1974, and 1975 respectively.

A combined effort is under way by the Ad Committee, IPHFHA, and PHI management to develop a more effective set of operating procedures and organizational guidelines for coordinated, cooperative local advertising and promotion programs.

As a result of the combined efforts of a national and local advertising sales promotion program and the development of new units, consumer awareness of Pizza Hut restaurants has risen significantly over the past four years to 98% (compared to 95% in November 1974) among our primary market (the 12–49-year-old group).

EXHIBIT 5-3:

PIZZA HUT:
CORPORATE STRATEGY

FROM THE BUSINESS PLAN OF PIZZA HUT

CORPORATE STRATEGY

What are the decisions needed today to make our business of tomorrow? Strategy determines whether or not we accomplish our plan in the most effective way. Our strategy needs to be general enough to allow specific supporting plans to be developed.

THE STRATEGY WE ARE USING IS A COMBINATION OF:

(These are forced ranked)

1.   Increasing the sales, profits, and productivity of the existing Pizza Hut system restaurants.

2.   Maintaining a solid financial base which gives us adequate financing.

3.   Continuing to build our base by developing new Pizza Hut restaurants for the optimum development of existing and new markets.

4.   Updating and modernizing the Pizza Hut system's restaurants to better compete in existing markets.

5.   Continuing the development and controlled growth of the international market.

6.   Continuing to expand our market penetration by building new pizza concepts.

7.   Continuing to sell or joint venture problem markets, areas, or restaurants.

8.   Increasing our penetration of the food away from home market by development, acquisition, and/or joint venture.

9.   Continuing the development of internal personnel and accelerating the selection and training of outside people for future management positions.

Marketing Issues: Who Are the Buyers?

A GRAPHIC DESIGNER who heads a thriving three-person business proudly told me that he doesn't do any marketing. That is, he explained, he uses no advertising or direct mail or public relations or other expensive gimmicks to get clients. Just high-quality work produced on time, he said.

So I asked him who his clients are. Mostly corporate personnel managers putting together recruitment brochures, he replied. And, I inquired, how does he find his clients? Well, he said, his clients come through referrals and word of mouth. And, oh yes, he also gives occasional talks to trade groups of corporate personnel managers.

I had to break the bad news to him that he does do marketing, as well as selling and promotion.

Marketing is something that every business owner does, even if he or she doesn't call it that. Marketing is, quite simply, *identifying your customer prospects and determining how best to reach them.* This designer served corporate personnel managers and reached them primarily through word-of-mouth referrals, along with the occasional speeches.

It's important to note, however, that marketing is *not* the same thing as selling or promoting. Those are separate tasks. Selling and promoting are essentially the implementation of your marketing plan. That is, once you have identified your customer prospects and determined how best to reach them, you then have to go out and make it happen. You make it happen through selling and promoting, which are covered in a separate section of the business plan—and of this book.

Clearly, you can't do an effective job of selling and promotion unless you have identified who you're selling to and how you can best reach the prospects to make your sales pitch. That up-front work requires the orderly accomplishment of several tasks, which are described in this chapter and become the basis of the marketing section of your business plan.

What Are You Selling?

This seems like a straightforward question. You're selling residential hardware or books or temporary personnel services or lawn care.

Asked another way—what are your customers buying?—this question might prompt a more detailed answer. A hardware store owner might say that customers are buying the best possible selection of hardware at the lowest possible prices. A temporary personnel firm might say it provides the most reliable and best-trained temporary secretaries at the most reasonable prices among competitors.

The only problem with such answers, though, is that competitors are saying similar things. A potential customer has no real way to distinguish you from the competition except to sample you both and make comparisons.

Such answers aren't unusual from entrepreneurs, since most invariably emphasize how wonderful their product or service is. After all, many companies originate as the result of a skill or hobby or work experience that involved a product or service. The founders understandably take pride in their ability to provide what they believe to be the best version of that product or service in the marketplace. In building a business, however, you need to sell benefits rather than products to your customers. You do that by identifying the benefits they will receive from your product or service. Mass-market consumer advertising promises all kinds of benefits. Eating high-fiber cereal or margarine will help you live longer. Using mouthwash will make you more popular. Buying a personal computer will make you more productive.

The marketing section of your business plan, then, should be focused on the *benefits* rather than on the *features* of your company's product or service.

The Best Benefits

The best benefits are those that favorably affect either people's feelings or their pocketbooks. Entrepreneurs who can express the market impact of their business in those terms usually have an advantage. For example, I read a local newspaper article about two women who had started a highly successful mail-order business selling clothing for overweight children. The children were thrilled with the product because of the difficulties—and the humiliation—they encountered shopping for clothes at traditional retail outlets. As one of the women observed, "What we're really selling is dignity for these children."

And so this company was. Sure, their clothing was of high quality and they delivered in a timely way. But the real reason for their success was they made children feel better. That pleased both the children and their parents.

Ironically, even businesses seemingly geared toward providing bargains are as much or more geared toward making people feel good. Retail discounters increasingly play on the feelings of satisfaction that people get when they save money on purchases. Thus, Filene's Basement stores use carrying bags that say in huge letters, "I JUST GOT A BARGAIN!"

In today's fast-paced environment, one of the critical benefits has come to be convenience. Products and services that save people time are often able to charge premium prices. We've seen the emergence of restaurant-delivery, home-cleaning, and party-planning services, not to mention the availability of just about anything through mail order, including stationery products, fresh flowers, and custom clothing.

Another way to view the idea of benefits—and to explain them in your business plan—is through the notion of adding value. What are you doing to the product or service you are selling that the customer couldn't easily do and that the customer values? Restaurants that offer delivery services are adding value by saving customers the time and energy associated with going out and picking up their take-out orders. One of the reasons that the concept of interactive television is so exciting to so many people during the mid-1990s is that it similarly offers some important values not available through existing businesses—either video rental stores or traditional cable television. By instantly calling up the movies of their choice on television, consumers could avoid trips to the video stores. Equally important, they could avoid the disappointment and frustration of discovering, after arriving at the video store, that the movie they wanted was unavailable.

Adding value has become important for every business, no matter how seemingly mundane its product or service. Indeed, it can be argued that the more mundane the product or service you are trying to sell, the more essential it is to figure out ways to add value. Thus, a small rock quarry in California has succeeded by continually finding ways to add value. It sorts the highest-quality crushed stone for customers. It is open for pickup of materials 24 hours a day—and fills the orders so the trucks are on their way in ten minutes. It responds immediately to customer problems and complaints. It also charges 5% to 10% more for its product than competitors do.

For business products, there's no better benefit to the customer than making or saving money. One of the reasons fax machines have become so popular is they became cost-effective. Once their cost was in the range of $500 to $1,000 or so, businesses could send many kinds of written communications faster than was possible using overnight delivery services, which cost from $10 to $20 each. People quickly calculated that they could pay for the fax machines after as little as 50 messages (allowing for the cost of the telephone calls, which for a typical long-distance fax message of two to four pages might be $1 to $3 each).

For a business that sent 20 messages monthly, the fax machine could pay for itself in less than three months. Thus, the machine could be portrayed as having a payback period for businesses of just under three months, and even less time by the mid-1990s. Similarly, if a $10,000 computer system enables you to do without a $20,000 per year employee, it pays for itself in six months. The sooner a client can pay for your service, the better—ideally within a year or else within two years.

The payback period approach can be applied to services as well. An interior designer specializing in working with businesses can offer these benefits:

• *Space.* Business designers can save their corporate clients 10% to 15% in space requirements through efficient design. Suppose, for instance, that an office building rents 10,000 square feet to a corporation at $35 a square foot. That 10,000 square feet costs $350,000. A 10% savings comes to $35,000.

If the designer charges a fee of $25,000, based on $2.50 a square foot, the payback period is in the neighborhood of eight to nine months.

• *Productivity.* If employees produce more because of improved lighting, furnishings, and decorations, the benefits can be calculated in dollars and cents. If productivity is assumed to increase by 5%, then take 5% of labor costs as the user benefit. Five percent of a $1-million payroll comes to $50,000 of labor savings, or $50,000 in productivity. If the design fee is $25,000, the payback period in this case is six months.

• *Savings on equipment and furnishings.* If a designer can obtain such items at lower prices than the competition because of his or her connections, then those savings can be quantified. The savings may equal or surpass the design fee.

Market Research: No Academic Exercise

Once you've identified customer benefits, you must determine if, indeed, enough customers exist to make your product/service profitable. That requires market research.

There's a tendency to think of market research as something very sophisticated and complicated, involving long surveys, regression analysis, and similar sorts of exercises. But market research is really a matter of learning two things:

1. Whether enough potential customers exist to enable your product or service to achieve the growth you're looking for;
2. Whether the industries you are going after are on the upswing or the decline.

Here are three key questions to guide you in your research:

1. What is the market, precisely? If you're selling restaurant supplies, are you selling to all restaurants or just fast-food restaurants or gourmet restaurants or wine bars? The more specific you can be, the better.

2. Is the market growing or shrinking? Obviously, you'll want a growing market rather than a declining market. Trying to sell typewriters in the face of the personal computer revolution has proven quite difficult. Someone considering getting into the liquor industry should think twice, since sales have been declining because of health and auto safety concerns.

3. Is it worth your while? You may have identified a growing niche market, but it may not achieve a size that makes it worthwhile. Consider the dilemma facing the owners of a company that markets a special massage tool (selling for $50) to physical therapists who deal with back problems. The market is growing and the tool is selling well. But the owners have encountered a problem. Even with growth, the physical therapist market is so small that nearly every person in it would have to buy the tool to make it worthwhile—a nearly impossible task no matter how good the product is. The owners' challenge is to identify other markets that might be able to use the tool, diversify, or face the prospect of a shrinking business.

Keep in mind. . . We are in an age of so-called market niches—a time when markets are becoming ever more narrow and precisely defined. Increasingly, providers of public relations services specialize in providing them exclusively to high-technology companies or to law firms. The days of mass production seem to be ending in favor of specialty marketers. Futurist Alvin Toffler refers to this change as "de-massification" of markets. Printers specialize in servicing users interested in long runs or short runs. Clothing makers target athletic women ages 20 to 35 and physical fitness centers target individuals 45 to 60. By virtue of serving niches, businesses are expected to be able to respond more quickly to changing customer tastes and needs. Your plan should point out the advantages you gain by targeting a particular niche.

Getting the Answers You Need

As I've noted, market research doesn't have to be complicated. Much of the information you need is available from public sources: government statistics, trade group surveys, computerized databases, and even the phone book.

Computerized databases have become so inclusive and accessible that many market research tasks can start by accessing CompuServe, Prodigy, or one of the other similar services and punching in the categories you would like information about. Many local libraries are plugged into databases and will do the work for you. The summaries of newspaper, magazine, and professional journal articles will often reveal important data, studies, competitors, experts, and other resources you can tap into. Such information can save you much time and many dead ends in your market research effort.

To appreciate how useful the phone book can be, consider the case of a wholesaler of cut flowers who wanted to explore the possibilities for selling flowers directly to large-scale users in the Boston area—caterers, funeral homes, restaurants, and so forth.

The first step was to consult the Yellow Pages and tally up the number of caterers, funeral homes, and restaurants. Next, the wholesaler obtained the number of weddings and deaths each year from a state census office.

From those statistics, it was possible to calculate the number of weddings per catering firm and funerals per funeral home. That data gave the wholesaler an idea of the total market for cut flowers in the region.

The next step was to do some test marketing, determining potential interest within the target market. The wholesaler contacted potential customers and tried out the user-benefit claims on them to determine what sparked interest and what didn't. The wholesaler discovered, to his surprise, a number of unanticipated barriers and he decided not to pursue the idea.

While the venture may appear to be a failure, I would suggest otherwise. Entrepreneurs shouldn't be afraid to take no for an answer from their market research. The last thing you want to do is fall blindly in love with your idea.

Keep in mind. . . Generally speaking, a do-it-yourself approach to market research is preferable to hiring an outside market research firm. For one thing, it's cheaper. For another, you'll often learn more than you expected by talking directly to prospects.

An exception to this advice would be a situation in which you need extensive consumer tests of a product or service. This is a complex area, and there are firms that specialize in doing surveys and interviews to gather such data.

Once your company is established, though, you often have more market data at your disposal than you realize by virtue of having serviced customers and listened to requests from prospects. The challenge is then to find an efficient and effective way of assembling the data from your staff.

Assessing the Competition

It's great to identify the benefits you can offer a growing and receptive market, but you have to keep in mind that you won't be operating in a vacuum. There's almost certainly competition for the market you've targeted. If there isn't, don't necessarily take that as a good sign. It may mean that the market isn't as receptive to your product or service as you think.

Entrepreneurs often take the competition too lightly. They assume that their own product or service is so much better than the competition's that there's no way customers won't make the obvious choice. The truth is that there are reasons that the competition is there and doing well, and you may not understand all those reasons.

Sometimes entrepreneurs think there's no competition, because they haven't looked deeply enough. The owner of a large brokerage service specializing in selling small businesses once observed, "Do you know who my biggest competitor is? It's FOSBY. That's 'for sale by owner.' " In other words, the competitor wasn't another business, but another means of doing business. For sellers of business services like graphic design, technical writing, and consulting, the real competition may be the preference of many companies to use in-house staff to perform the service.

Whatever the situation, the business plan should explicitly take account of the competition—listing competitors and explaining their strengths and weaknesses.

In addition, the business plan should explain what the company will do to exceed and stay ahead of the competition. Will the company provide faster turnaround times? Offer higher-quality materials? Sell the same services at a lower price via use of new technology? Offer new services? In other words, how will the company go about achieving and maintaining what is sometimes referred to as a competitive advantage?

In a global economy, competitive advantages are more important than ever. You never know where new competitors will come from. Only one thing is certain: they will continually crop up. Part of your job in the business plan is to make a case for your company to stay a step ahead of the competition.

Putting the Marketing Plan to Paper: The Ben & Jerry's Model

Once you have taken the steps described in this chapter, you should be able to make a convincing case for the market you have chosen—convincing to you and to potential investors, executives, and others. Clearly, if your company is well established, you'll have an easier time making your case because you will know which market segments have bought most and which least. But even with such experience, you must still make projections for the future; that can be as tricky for an established business as for a start-up.

The section of Ben & Jerry's business plan describing the market for its two products—packaged ice cream and ice cream shops (referred to as scoop shops)—illustrates the kind of data that should be included in the marketing plan (see Exhibit 6–1). It begins by describing the size of the American ice cream market and its growth rate. It then shows that the superpremium ice cream market segment is growing at a significantly faster rate than the total market, having risen from 11% to 20% of the market in one year.

This description of the market helps explain the more than 100% annual growth of Ben & Jerry's in the New England market, as discussed in the second paragraph. There's no need to begin explaining the customer benefit because, clearly, that's coming across to buyers.

Ben & Jerry's next demonstrates that demand is so intense—for both new scoop shops and franchises—that the company has been turning away business. This information helps justify the need for investment funds so that the company can expand to accommodate the demand—which is the purpose of the plan.

The plan next describes negotiations for both scoop shops and franchises. This information shows that the company is taking advantage of whatever growth potential is allowable within its existing financial constraints.

Assessing the Competition: The Pizza Hut Model

Of all the business plans I examined, Pizza Hut's contained the most extensive analysis of the competition (see Exhibit 6–2). The plan points out that the company's competition extends beyond other pizza chains to "all grocery stores and/or outlets where food away from home may be purchased." It next assesses the number of outlets and sales performance of eating places falling into its segment of outlets—those doing $100,000 to $300,000 in annual business each.

Finally, it briefly discusses four of its major competitors, noting the strength of Pizza Inn and the weaknesses of the others. Even executives as savvy as those at Pizza Hut aren't infallible, though. Note the mention of Domino's as one of several showing "little overt activity in 1975." That's one competitor that didn't get as much attention as it should have.

CHAPTER SIX

EXERCISES

Worksheets for this chapter are provided on page 218

1. List your product's or service's three principal customer benefits.

2. Identify three sources of market research.

3. Identify your top two competitors and explain the primary strengths and weaknesses of each.

4. Describe at least two ways in which your company will gain a competitive advantage over the top competitors you have identified.

EXHIBIT 6-1:

BEN & JERRY'S:
ASSESSING THE COMPETITION

SCOPE OF THE MARKET

The size of the total ice cream market in the United States is approximately 851 million gallons per year and is growing at the rate of 1–2 percent per year. The size of the ice cream market in New England is approximately 65 million gallons per year. The size of the superpremium segment of the national frozen desserts market grew from 11 percent in 1981 to 20 percent in 1982.

The Company has been growing in the New England market at a rate of over 100 percent per year during the most recent three-year period.

Vroman Foods, Natural Nectar, and Haagen Dazs have demonstrated that it is feasible to ship to all 50 states from a single ice cream plant. Although there can be no assurance, management believes that the Company can enter many new markets and garner a percentage of the "superpremium" market in that area. For example, the Company presently sells approximately 5,000 gallons of Ben & Jerry's ice cream, per month, in the greater Boston market.

The Company currently has seven scoop shops. A scoop shop is a retail ice cream parlor. The scoop shop in Burlington, Vermont, is Company owned. The other six are franchised, and located in Portland, Maine; Essex Junction and Shelburne, Vermont; and Albany, Schenectady, and Saratoga Springs, New York. The growth of the franchised scoop shop division has deliberately been limited by the Company in order to develop the necessary systems, personnel, and products, prior to expansion.

The two most recently opened scoop shops, a renovated freestanding building in Schenectady, New York, and a 250-square-foot walk-up in Crossgates Mall (Pyramid Co.) in Albany, New York, are projected to generate gross sales of $300,000 per year and $400,000 per year, respectively. Pyramid Mall in Holyoke, Massachusetts, and Clifton County Mall in Clifton Park, New York, are currently seeking to persuade the Company to establish Ben & Jerry's scoop shops on their properties.

The Company is currently in contract negotiation with a regional franchisee who plans to open ten franchised Ben & Jerry's scoop shops in the greater Boston area during the next three years, although there can be no assurance that the negotiations will successfully be concluded. Negotiations are also under way with franchisees for sites in Plattsburg, New York, and Concord, New Hampshire, although there can be no assurance that the negotiations will successfully be concluded.

The Company is presently conducting a search for a Director of Retail Operations to expand the franchised Scoop Shop division. Management expects the successful candidate will have multiunit ice cream food service experience.

Aside from increasing its share of the market in New England, the Company presently plans to enter new markets in New York, New Jersey, Washington, Florida, and Montreal with distribution of pints to grocery stores and franchised scoop shops. The Company anticipates that if its business plan is implemented in accordance with the present timetable (see "Projections" and "Use of Proceeds"), in 1992 it will be able to satisfy five percent of the national market and twenty-five percent of the New England market for "superpremium" ice cream.

The Company offers franchised scoop shops at an initial franchise fee of $12,600. In addition, the franchisee pays to the Company an advertising fee of four percent of the franchisees' total gross sales. The fee is used to defray the cost of regional and local advertising. The typical franchise agreement calls for the franchise to purchase various products exclusively from the Company. The Company derives income from sales made by it directly to the franchisee. A franchise agreement is typically for a ten-year term with an option to renew the franchise for an additional ten-year term.

EXHIBIT 6-2:

PIZZA HUT:
ASSESSING THE COMPETITION

COMPETITIVE ANALYSIS

We must define our competition according to the customer's concept of what product or service he will buy. After we know who is providing this—what their relative strengths and weaknesses are—what their projected development might be. . . then we must ask ourselves: "HOW DO WE POSITION OURSELVES IN THE MARKETPLACE?"

While our primary competition is often thought of in terms of other pizza chains, it should be remembered that in reality we compete for that portion of income that is allocated to food. . . hence our competition is all grocery stores and/or outlets where food away from home may be purchased.

In July 1973, the consumer price index for food away from home reached a level equal to food at home prices. With the exception of the March–May 1975 period, the index has reflected an advantage to eating away from home versus at home. This awareness has resulted in the fact that it is now stated that one in every three dollars spent on food is spent away from home, with the predictions that this figure will rise to one out of every two dollars.

In terms of all eating and drinking establishments, calendar 1974 indicated that real monthly sales gains overall were down over the previous year. During 1975, this trend has been reversed, with real sales gains returning to levels comparable to years previous to 1974.

Additionally, based on hard data now available for the years 1963–1972 the trend within the eating place market gives us further insights into what is occurring in the marketplace:

PIZZA HUT: ASSESSING THE COMPETITION
continued

Annual Volume	% of all Units		% of Total Sales	
	1963	**1972**	**1963**	**1972**
Less than $100,000	84.0	66.0	40.0	20.0
$100,000 to $300,000	13.0	24.0	32.0	33.0
$300,000 to $500,000	2.0	6.0	12.0	18.0
$500,000 to $1 million	1.0	3.3	10.0	18.0
$1 million +	0.3	0.8	6.0	10.5

NOTE: Due to rounding, percentages may not equal 100.0

Within our segment of the business (basically the $100,000 to $300,000 range), the numbers of units increased dramatically from 24,230 to 53,483, as did the percentage of all units from 13% to 24%, and yet the percentage of all units, total sales remained relatively constant for this group. In summary, the trend is definitely toward significantly larger establishments.

With the pizza segment of the food away from home, we will overview some of the larger national/regional systems and touch upon others in the marketplace mentioned in previous years.

PIZZA INN

Our observations of this Dallas-based chain indicate that 1975 was basically a year of further entrenching its position in the Dallas-Ft.Worth complex, as well as the areas of West Texas, while slowly expanding the chain through random franchise activities elsewhere. The company has continued a heavy concentration in both media and promotional efforts in Dallas-Ft.Worth and has begun testing implementation of an "old-fashioned pizza," which is a thick-style pizza, in addition to its thin version.

SHAKEY'S

Again this year, the activities of this Denver-based chain continue to be sporadic. After the Hunt Brothers acquired the company from Great Western, many of its executive personnel, including the President, have left. The prototype "pizza in the round" walkup concept tested in Denver has been closed (development very spotty and rumored future as to ownership in doubt). During the year we evidenced an introduction in certain units of "Skilletti," a spaghetti in a skillet product, and the company is testing a pizza-by-the-ounce format in certain select units.

VILLAGE INN

Concentration in 1975 seemed to be centered around the home market of Metro Phoenix. In response to our introduction of Thick 'n Chewy, Village Inn began implementation of a deep-pan-type product. Our indications are that it experienced difficulties with the product, retrenched and reformulated, and is now implementing a newer version of a thick-type product in the Phoenix area stores.

STRAW HAT

Indications are that Straw Hat is in the process of trying to sublease its operations outside the state of California, which would support observations that its entries into non-California markets have been less than successful. At the same time, a new prototype has opened in Concord, California, which is surprisingly similar in basics to our Applegate's. An existing unit in Concord was closed and totally remodeled. Initial observations indicate a greater degree of customer acceptance than the original concept offered. Again, 1975 could be expressed as a year of retrenchment and perhaps a redirection of positioning within the pizza market.

For the remainder of other entries in the pizza-oriented marketplace such as Ken's, Pasquale's, Domino's, Cassano's, Round Table, etc., there has been little overt activity in 1975. The economic uncertainties of 1975 may have led to uncertainty as to future direction.

6

Marketing Issues:
Who Are
the Buyers?

Product/Service Issues: What Are You Selling?

MOST ENTREPRENEURS are very proud of their products and/or services and believe that their value is what determines the company's success. Certainly all the attention in recent years given to the quality of American products versus those of foreign companies underscores the importance of having pride in your product or service.

I don't mean to suggest that the emphasis on product features and quality is wrong. Rather, I believe it is misguided for many companies because it throws their entrepreneurs off target in terms of the planning process and the written plan. Two issues are primary in viewing the product or service:

1. The market and what it values should determine the particulars of the product or service. The owners of a company that arranges auto repair services for corporate owners of large fleets and has $3 million in annual sales decided to develop a new software product that would remind the fleet owners about the need to do such regular maintenance as oil changes and tune-ups. The company invested $200,000 in developing and attempting to sell the product before realizing that low-level fleet managers didn't have the authority to commit their companies to the product, which might cost $50,000 annually for a fleet of several thousand cars. Getting in to make a sales pitch to high-level financial executives proved extremely difficult.

In their desperation to salvage the product, the fleet repair company's owners decided that auto dealers might welcome the maintenance reminders as a service they could sell to individual consumers. But this time, before launching the product, the owners hired a market research firm to confirm that interest really existed. They discovered that auto dealers liked it not only because they could sell it as an additional service but also because it encouraged consumers to use the dealership for oil changes and other work. And consumers liked it because it kept their warranties valid.

Suddenly, the same product, which had been rejected by one market, was adopted enthusiastically by another. The business owners learned an important lesson: let the market determine your product characteristics. They also came to appreciate the importance of planning since the process of putting together a written plan would have alerted them much earlier to the need for market research.

2. Given the fact that a market exists and is prepared to buy, can you deliver what you promise in a timely and cost-effective way? One of the worst things a business can do is to identify a viable market, obtain orders, and then fail to produce the product or service on time or meet the quality standards expected by customers or adhere to the price quoted. This has been a notorious problem in the computer software industry. Prominent companies announce that new products will be available on a certain date and then don't deliver because of snags in the development process. They then must announce delays, which naturally undermines their credibility with customers. These companies are large and prosperous enough that they can absorb the losses, but smaller companies often can't.

Even worse is to deliver on time but come out with a flawed product. I know of one case in which a maker of a special component for refrigerators delivered a new version to a major appliance manufacturer, which then discovered that the component was flawed. The appliance manufacturer canceled its orders and the small components company was nearly thrown into bankruptcy.

People Express encountered difficulties in its early days because demand for its services was so great that its phone reservations system, airline capacity, and other functions couldn't handle the load. Video footage of unhappy travelers at Newark and other airports on the evening news didn't help the upstart airline's growth process. While People Express survived, entrepreneurs should be aware that failure to plan adequately for such problems can lead to the downfall of an otherwise viable business.

Clearly, then, marketing and product issues are closely related. The relationship of these issues varies somewhat depending on the company's stage of development (see the box on page 118). In considering the product/service section of the plan, here are issues that must be addressed:

1. Product/service features: How many bells and whistles?

Here you want to determine exactly what your product or service consists of. You can best do this by asking yourself a series of questions about what you include and don't include in your basic offering.

For instance, if you are offering interior design services for businesses, do you also make available architectural services? Do you help buy furniture and fixtures for clients? Do you provide follow-up consultation after the initial design is complete? If the answers are yes, do you include these services in your basic design package or do you charge separately?

If you are making a food product for retail sale, do you rely on dehydrated ingredients or use more expensive and fragile fresh ingredients? Do you use easy-open packaging? Do you provide a call-in service for consumers with questions or complaints?

Entrepreneurs naturally want to produce the best possible product or offer the best possible service they can. They are aware of the increasing emphasis being placed on quality and of the intensity of the competition's desire to please customers. At the same time, you can fall into the trap of trying to offer too much. Makers of technology products often make this mistake as their engineers try to build in as many options and features as possible. The problems arise when, first, the product isn't completed on time and, second, when its cost is higher than expected.

In composing the business plan, you must explore two points about features in depth. You should begin by listing the major ones your product or service incorporates. You may think you've got them all in your head, but the task of writing them down is often revealing. Suddenly, you may realize that you're trying to do too much or too little. Or you may find that you're not sure a particular gadget or service is really necessary, given its cost.

In the latter situation, you may find yourself going back to the marketplace or to your salespeople for answers. Sometimes, a more comfortable handle on a carrying case or a clearer instruction sheet accompanying a product can be very important to the buyer—and inexpensive to add. On the other hand, features you thought were important—and are expensive—may turn out to be unimportant to the buyer.

2. Price: High enough, but not too high.

Pricing is one of the trickiest areas of business for small companies and major corporations alike. An inexperienced manager might suppose that simple formulas exist for determining price—say, a certain multiple of costs.

Certainly you can begin calculating a price range as a function of your costs. Indeed, your final price must provide a substantial enough margin over your costs to allow for taxes and profit. (Cash flow and other financial issues stemming from price are discussed at length in Chapter 9.)

The issue of price is a controversial one; business school professors disagree over which factors are most important in determining price. The reality is that price is a function of several interrelated factors:

• **What customers will pay.** In doing your market research and test marketing, you should have gotten feedback on price. Presumably, you tested your product or service at a few prices and sensed where you began to encounter resistance and where volume could be expected to go up significantly.

• **What the competition is charging.** Certainly if your prices are significantly above or below those charged by competitors, prospects are going to wonder why. If your product or service outperforms the competition, then a higher price may be warranted. Or if you've come up with a way to lower production costs, you may be able to win customers by undercutting the competition. Beware on this last point, however. In many markets, such as consulting and public relations, customers are wary of low-price producers, fearing reduced quality.

• **What the effects of product or service features are on price.** Figure in your costs and determine, based on what you know about the market, whether they're essential. As I've noted, some special service feature, such as 24-hour turnaround on product delivery, may not be all that important to customers. In the case of a product like Ben & Jerry's ice cream, on the other hand, the expense of premium ingredients is used to justify top-of-the-line prices.

Keep in mind. . . Pricing is a tough decision. Remember that whatever prices you arrive at for your product line aren't engraved in stone. In some industries, like electronics and clothing, sellers tend to start high and gradually cut their prices over time. In others, particularly industrial supplies and parts, prices tend to gradually rise over time. One thing to avoid is going in the opposite direction of what is common in your industry—for example, if you lower prices in an industry where they tend to rise, customers may perceive it as a sign of desperation.

3. Production: Can you get the product or service out?

There's no better way to turn off prospective or existing customers than failing to deliver the product or service you promised. Product companies often suffer from "a backlog problem." As the backlog stretches out from weeks to months, customers begin to cancel orders if other options exist. Suddenly, the backlog evaporates and all the investment that's been made in equipment and people is wasted.

The problem affects service companies as well. Consider the case of a company that provides specialized training to personnel managers of major corporations on handling AIDS and drug problems. Demand for its services was soaring, but it didn't have enough trainers. Finding and training specialists took months, and the company lost out on profitable opportunities. More thorough market research probably would have helped the company manage this situation, perhaps by raising investment funds to pay for hiring and training the new presenters earlier in the company's life.

4. Warranties/repairs: Who will provide ongoing service?

One challenge faced by smaller companies, particularly makers of products, is persuading the prospective buyer that they will be around for the long term to provide ongoing service—repairs, replacement parts, and updated products. The business plan must address the issue of ongoing service, both to determine its exact form and to allow for the costs of providing it.

The first concern that typically arises is that of a warranty. How complete is the warranty and how long should it extend? That is, does the warranty cover parts and labor, or just parts? Does it extend for six months, one year, or two years? Obviously, the more complete and lengthy the warranty, the more costly it will be.

Warranty decisions should be driven by factors similar to those that determine price—how important the warranty is to the market, what competitors are doing, how the costs come out. Concerning costs, providing in-house labor may be very expensive, whereas subcontracting out repairs could be much less costly.

■ With Growth Comes Larger Product Issues

The start-up company and the established company must view the product issue from different vantage points.

For the start-up company, the biggest unknown is whether a market really exists for the product or service under consideration. Therefore, the business plan must demonstrate convincingly that a market truly exists. Software Publishing's business plan thus focuses on marketing issues rather than on the details of producing personal computer software.

For the established company, the existence of a market is a given. More important is where market growth will come from and what products or services the company has to satisfy that growth.

The business plans for companies like Celestial Seasonings and Pizza Hut devote many pages to assessing their product lines. We see which tea flavors are most popular and which are least popular and what can be done to reverse the fortunes of the laggards. There's no need to establish that significant markets exist for herbal tea and pizza or that these companies have discovered formulas to satisfy the marketplace. The key issues are which products and distribution methods will allow for continuing growth.

The next concern is additional service. If it's important that customers be able to buy certain replacement parts, will your company stock them? Or will your company provide repair services? If the answer to these questions is yes, then you must decide if such services will be provided at cost to maintain customer loyalty or if you want them to be profitable in and of themselves.

For companies that expect to come out with improved versions of their basic product, another issue is how those later versions will be devised. Will your company do the development in house and, if so, how much will you spend? Or will you subcontract work out? Or will you put off development until you get closer to the time when the improved version is necessary?

Top management must address these issues and explain them in the business plan.

Addressing the Key Service Issues: The People Express Model

While I pointed out earlier that People Express had encountered problems when demand for its services turned out to be greater than anticipated, its business plan did an excellent job of itemizing the most relevant service issues—and how they would affect operations. These issues include the number of aircraft required, the best types, their configuration, prices, and scheduling (see Exhibit 7–1). Indeed, as the business plan suggests, the operating approach—its service features and their costs—is the key to this company's financial success.

Thus, the plan notes that planes will use oversized storage racks and seats designed to hold a maximum amount of luggage underneath. The company used that point in its advertising to explain how that helped keep fares down. The business plan backs that up by saying that the purpose was to "minimize the need for luggage in the hold, resulting in quick turnaround operations requiring less manpower and ground equipment and most importantly, short ground times."

The business plan goes on to list seven operational factors that will enable the company to maximize revenues and profits. These include high-density seating, low investment in on-ground facilities, and so forth. Once again, service design becomes key to the company's overall strategy. By eliminating frills and the heavy fixed expenses common to competitors (extensive ground facilities, management bureaucracy), People Express can cut its costs and, most important from a marketing perspective, its prices.

And so it worked out in practice. The flying public could equate the big on-board baggage bins and high-density seating with the bargain-basement prices the company promoted. The operation was intrinsically tied into the marketing strategy, even if the business plan didn't state it quite so boldly.

Assessing the Key Product Issues: The Ben & Jerry's Model

In Ben & Jerry's offering statement, the product's key ingredients are discussed. But note that they are considered almost entirely in relationship to the competition (see Exhibit 7–2). Thus, the fact that its ice cream uses pure cane sugar is noted by describing what the competition does: "Most other ice creams use some form of corn syrup or corn syrup solids." The company points out that no fillers are used because competitors rely on fillers.

Technology is important as well, the business plan states: "Perfecting the technique of inserting large chunks of cookies and candies into ice cream has required a considerable investment in research and design and the purchase of new machinery and its subsequent modification." And the need for quality control is acknowledged, if only briefly.

EXERCISES

Worksheets for this chapter are provided on page 220

1. List the four most important features of your company's main product or service.

2. List the four least important features of your company's main product or service.

3. Determine which of the least important features is most costly. How necessary is that feature?

4. Relate in three or four sentences how your company would respond if demand for your company's product or service sharply exceeded your expectations.

5. Describe in three or four sentences your company's plans for providing after-sales service.

Products/Services:
What Are
You Selling?

EXHIBIT 7-1:

PEOPLE EXPRESS:
ASSESSING SERVICE ISSUES

Operations

It is projected that initial operations will commence June 1, 1981, with three aircraft. This will allow the first-stage network to connect at least four cities a minimum of three times per day for commuter markets and in most cases four times. Additionally, sufficient equipment time will be available to provide service to a fourth city on a minimal basis to provide access to a leisure destination such as Miami or Ft. Lauderdale.

The three aircraft will generate about 10 hours per day utilization. With an average hop of about 300 miles this will generate 3,000 plane miles per day per plane. The resulting statistics are displayed below:

The aircraft assumed in this case are of the DC-9-30 or 737-200 type, the stretched version of the basic aircraft. These aircraft can be fitted with beverage galleys, oversized storage racks, and seats designed to hold a maximum amount of luggage underneath. This will minimize the need for luggage in the hold, resulting in quick turnaround operations requiring less manpower and ground equipment and most importantly, short ground times.

Assuming the average cost of operations on a fully allocated basis to be about $2,000 per hour (or $6.67 per mile), the cost per day for the three-plane network would be:

> 10 hours X 3 planes X $2,000 = $60,000
> or $1.8 million per month, or $21,600,000 per year

An average fare of just $40 per passenger is equivalent to a yield of 11.7¢ per revenue seat mile, a bargain at today's rates. Even allowing for a 10% error factor, this still results in a yield of only 12.8¢ and hourly costs of $2,200 per hour, which is still well below current competition. At this rate, the company needs 57 passengers per segment to break even or a low 47.6% load factor. Above that level, 90% of all revenues would drop to the bottom line due to the highly leveraged nature of air transportation. One of the company's objectives would be to use its relative cost advantages to the utmost and price its product in such a way as to maximize profits. On a conservative basis, this means operating at a projected load factor of about 60%, which leaves a comfortable margin for unknown factors such as price increases or lessened demand. At a margin of 60% load factor or 72 passengers per flight, the airline will net $2,520 per hour compared with $2,000 per hour in fully allocated costs for a 26% return on sales.

The ability of this kind of operation to generate these revenues at lower costs is clear. Among the advantages:

1) High-density seating, 120 seats compared with 95 at most carriers, with comfort
2) New personnel with many comparative advantages
3) Greatly reduced investment in physical assets such as ground equipment and facilities
4) Simple systems and procedures
5) Streamlined management
6) Equipment designed for routes flown
7) No coat closets, no galleys, no freight, no mail, and no interlining*, etc.

Flight Equipment:

Aircraft for the type of operations herein envisioned would be of the two-engine type such as the DC-9 or B-737. These aircraft are ideally suited for hauls of from 150 to 1,200 miles and are highly economic. They have two engines and need but two pilots to operate. They are self-contained units requiring little ground support equipment. The dispatch reliability of both types are the highest in commercial aviation, resulting in little down-time and high dependability. They are relatively lightweight, resulting in low landing fees. Additionally, their very commonness makes them easy to repair. Of course, all aircraft acquired will be of the same type to minimize training and provisioning.

Used aircraft are constantly coming to the market as carriers change their fleet mix to reflect their changing needs. For example, United is currently disposing of its B-737 fleet while TWA is doing likewise with its DC-9's. Therefore, availability of good used equipment is no problem.

The initial order for equipment should encompass ten aircraft, the first three to be delivered in sufficient time to initiate operations by June 1, 1981. Follow-on deliveries would be spaced over the next eighteen months.

* Transfer of passengers and baggage between companies

EXHIBIT 7-2:

BEN & JERRY'S:
ASSESSING PRODUCT ISSUES

PRODUCT AND MARKETING

The growth of the Company, to date, has been due in large part to the quality of the product and the development of an effective marketing technique.

(1) The Product.

Ben & Jerry's ice cream is a high (15.2%) fat ice cream. This fat is derived mostly from the butterfat in cream but also from egg yolks. The ice cream contains at least 1.5% egg yolk solids which technically classifies it as one of the few "French Ice Creams" manufactured in the United States, as defined by Federal Law.

The ice cream also contains a high amount of milk solids, which (along with the product's low overrun) tends to give Ben & Jerry's ice cream more body than most other ice creams.

Pure cane sugar is the sweetening agent used in Ben & Jerry's ice cream. Most other ice creams use some form of corn syrup or corn syrup solids.

There are no fillers in Ben & Jerry's ice cream. Many other ice creams use whey or sodium-cassinates and corn syrup derivatives.

Ben & Jerry's ice cream itself contains no artificial ingredients and no preservatives. (Some cookies and candies [Oreos and Heath Bars] used in some Ben & Jerry's ice cream do contain artificial ingredients, chemicals, and preservatives.)

The Company's ice cream is highly flavored. The theory behind this is that a consumer should be able to tell what flavor he or she is eating by how it tastes and not by how it is artificially colored. The flavorings used by the Company include premium quality, unpreserved extracts and fruits, nut meats, chocolates, liqueurs, and some cookies and candies.

The unusual flavor selection is what sets Ben & Jerry's ice cream apart from many other ice creams. Management believes there is no other "superpremium" ice cream that offers ice cream flavors such as: Heath Bar Crunch, Mint with Oreo Cookies, Dastardly Mash, or White Russian. Perfecting the technique of inserting large chunks of cookies and candies into ice cream has required a considerable investment in research and design and the purchase of new machinery and its subsequent modification.

The Company recently initiated a "rotating feature flavor" program. The first feature flavor, White Russian, became so popular that the Company decided to keep it as a permanent flavor.

(2) Quality Control.

The new plant will be equipped with a quality control laboratory and a quality control technician whose major responsibility will be the maintenance of the Company's existing standards of quality.

Products/Services: What Are You Selling

7

Sales and Promotion Issues: How Do You Sell?

YOU'VE IDENTIFIED user benefits, done your market research, assessed the competition, defined your product, and made sure you can produce and service it. Now you have to decide how you will sell your product and/or service.

This is really the second half of the marketing agenda—the implementation half, and the toughest half. It's the key to everything else in the business. Everything in the business can be carefully prepared, from the management team to the product quality to the financial projections, but without a way to close on orders, it's all meaningless.

Once you've identified your customer benefits as described in the previous chapter, selling and promotion become a matter of communicating those benefits to prospective customers effectively enough that they buy. At first glance, selling seems like a straightforward task. If you've been in business for a while, you already have a selling approach. And if you're just starting out in business, you have some idea of how the competition does its selling or what the usual sales approaches are in your industry.

But as any experienced entrepreneur knows, that's not enough. Your sales effort must be cost-effective. Keeping the salespeople from getting discouraged is another challenge. Getting the attention of prospects and customers in the daily clutter of advertising, television and radio programs, and direct mail is increasingly difficult. And demonstrating previous success can be tricky.

Indeed, selling is probably the most challenging of all issues you must deal with in most businesses. As such, it's a tough one to handle in writing the business plan. You can get at it, though, by providing persuasive answers to four questions:

1. What Is Your Selling Approach?

Do you plan to hire a sales force? Or use sales representatives? Or telemarketing? Or direct mail? Or retail outlets?

The answers may seem self-evident, based on your past experience or your knowledge of your industry. Celestial Seasonings sells its tea through supermarkets and other food retailers. Pizza Hut sells its pizza through freestanding fast-food restaurants. And People Express (now part of Continental Airlines) sells its tickets primarily via travel agencies, airport ticket counter locations, and over the phone.

Increasingly, though, creative entrepreneurs are looking for alternative sales approaches. Thus, a Boston-area maker of stereo products decided to avoid the traditional retail outlets and sell a new compact stereo system door to door with its own sales force. The firm avoided the crowded retail shelves and kept margins higher than discount-minded retailers will allow. A number of distributors of women's clothing have been extremely successful selling via direct-mail catalogs rather than through traditional retail boutiques. And Home Shopping Network became very successful selling traditional department store goods through a nonstop television show.

Two forces are driving these efforts. First and foremost, sales costs have risen dramatically in recent years. Having your own salesperson making personal visits to potential customers can cost $200 or more each, based on travel, salary, and other expenses. Not even the best salesperson will succeed with every prospect, so the cost of each completed sale can easily be $600, $800, or $1,000, depending on the salesperson's "hit rate."

Direct-mail costs have risen dramatically as well. Bulk-mail postage rates alone have risen nearly 50% in recent years. That doesn't take into account rising printing, stuffing, and other costs.

Second, competition within many sales outlets has become incredibly intense. Just getting a new food product onto supermarket shelves, even for a well-established company, can be nearly impossible. In some cases, supermarkets are charging expensive premiums—beyond the affordability of most smaller companies—simply to place particular products on their shelves. Direct-mail volume rises every year, making it difficult for mail-order companies to get their catalogs noticed.

Selling guidelines. Companies should expect to spend about 10% of their revenues on sales. Anything above that will likely become burdensome. Of course, there's nothing wrong with keeping the costs below 10%.

With that as a goal, it quickly becomes apparent that certain products or services have limited sales approaches. High-ticket industrial products selling for $50,000 or $60,000 each can justify the involvement of high-level executives in the sales process. But $1,000 fax machines must be sold via retail or mail-order outlets.

Here are the primary sales approaches:

• *Executive selling.* For high-ticket items—usually in excess of $50,000—the company's president may go out on sales calls and spend half a day or more with particularly promising prospects. This happens in fields like corporate consulting, where contracts may well exceed $100,000. Sales of such services understandably aren't made after one visit, but usually over a period of weeks or months. The executive involvement is necessary to win the potential customer's trust.

- *In-house sales force.* Supporting an in-house sales force can be quite expensive, with the cost of each sale running $1,000 or more. That makes it necessary to have a product/service selling price of $10,000 or sell in quantities totaling at least $10,000. For products that sell in large quantities to certain segments, an in-house sales force can be used only for those segments. For example, food products may sell in large quantities to institutional customers (hospitals, corporate cafeterias) and in small quantities to supermarkets and convenience stores. So an in-house sales force would be used for the institutional customers and another, less expensive sales approach would be used for the noninstitutional customers.

- *Sales representatives.* These are usually either manufacturers' representatives, brokers, wholesalers, distributors, or other commissioned part-time salespeople. They are part time because they represent several companies and divide their sales costs among a number of products. Thus, they are most appropriate for products that typically sell for between $1,000 and $10,000. The main difference between types of representatives is determined by whether they take possession of the products they sell. Wholesalers and distributors do take possession, while brokers and manufacturers' representatives act only as intermediaries. The difference becomes important in determining inventory storage, shipping, and other costs.

- *Mass distribution.* This includes primarily retailing, direct mail, and telemarketing. Products that sell for less than $1,000—clothing, consumer appliances, magazine subscriptions, sporting goods, and so on—are sold through mass-distribution outlets. This is probably the most crowded and intensely competitive of the sales approaches available and must be carefully planned. A clothing product that isn't displayed prominently by retailers or a direct-mail catalog that isn't handled properly by postal authorities because of incorrect sizing or metering can be terribly costly.

Of course, there is some overlap among these categories. For instance, personal computers, televisions, jewelry, and other items that sell for more than $1,000 are sold through mass-distribution channels, while home furnishings, cosmetics, and other items that often cost less than $1,000 may be sold direct to consumers by distributors. The following table summarizes the four main sales approaches:

Sales Approach	Price Range	Product/Service
Executive Selling	More than $50,000	Major medical equipment, electric power generators, consulting services
In-House Sales Force	$10,000–$50,000	Minicomputers, electronic instrumentation, industrial cleaning contracts
Sales Representatives	$1,000–$10,000	Packaged foods, industrial flooring, minicomputer software
Mass Distribution	Under $1,000	Consumer electronics, clothing, newsletter subscriptions

2. How Will You Motivate Your Sellers?

Selling is tough. Salespeople have to be able to deal with endless rejection and still remain positive and enthusiastic. Moreover, they must be able to make professional presentations, answer questions, handle complex requests, and otherwise turn prospects into customers.

Clearly, then, simply deciding which sales avenue you plan to use isn't the end of the planning process. The business plan must discuss how you will motivate your salespeople. Here are three tasks that must be dealt with:

1. Training. The salespeople, whether they're your own or representatives, must be thoroughly familiar with your product or service. That means they must understand how it works, what its benefits are, and how to sell it most effectively. If the product is going to be updated frequently, the salespeople need to be informed about the changes.

Even retailers and telemarketing people need to be trained. That may mean either visiting retailers or bringing groups into your company from retail outlets. In some cases, they can be educated via printed material, videotapes, and other means.

Two points are relevant here. First, training costs money, which must be allowed for in the business plan. Second, expect that the better trained the sales force is, the better it will perform. If you try to skimp in this area, it will probably show up in disappointing results.

2. Support. Your salespeople need a variety of materials to do an effective job of selling—brochures, presentation slides or overheads, samples, and so forth. In addition, one or more management officials should be available to answer questions from salespeople about things like product capabilities, delivery times, and warranties.

3. Incentives. This is a sensitive, controversial issue. Many management experts feel strongly that salespeople should work entirely on a commission basis. Others feel that salespeople should be partially on commission and partially salaried, to restrain their tendency to slash prices and otherwise make special deals to move products.

Most management experts agree that salespeople (or organizations, such as distributors or retailers) need incentives in the form of commissions, bonuses, prizes, and other inducements. The challenge comes in structuring incentives so that they benefit both the salesperson and the company. If they're too restrictive or inadequate, the incentives won't motivate as intended. If they're too generous, the incentives will become more expensive than the company can afford, leaving management in the uncomfortable position of having to cut back—which is a sure prescription for demotivating salespeople.

3. How Will You Promote Your Product or Service?

Creating a public image has become an essential part of any sales effort. Advertising and promotion/public relations are usually the means of making this happen.

Advertising is fairly straightforward. You decide where you want your business to advertise, determine the rates, and calculate the costs. For well-established companies, advertising can be very important, and the business plan should account for how much will be spent.

For start-up and early-stage companies, advertising is often too costly. Fortunately, promotion and public relations are much like home remodeling—they can be done either by outside professionals or by business owners on a do-it-yourself basis. When done in the latter way, the cash outlay can be minimal. Of course, even companies that advertise are well advised to use promotion and public relations techniques. What follows are some approaches for planning your promotion and public relations effort as part of the sales section of the business plan.

Promotional opportunities. The beautiful thing about promotion is that you can be a one-person show and give the impression of being a substantial company. How do you do that? By using the media. If your company is written up favorably in a newspaper or magazine article, you gain much more credibility than you do through any advertising. And best of all, it's free. The first step in effective promotion is targeting which market you want to reach and determining which media reach it.

If you want to reach plastics manufacturers, there are several magazines and newsletters targeted to that market. If you want to reach the personnel employment agency market, you will find a number of publications that serve that market.

Indeed, for any industry you can name, there are invariably several magazines and/or newsletters being read by major players in that field.

Will they take your material? Believe it or not, editors are looking for stories and are sometimes desperate for stories. Having worked on that side of the fence, I can tell you that the deadlines never let up. There's always the next issue to fill, and many entrepreneurs are pleasantly surprised by how easy it is to get articles into a trade publication.

Another potentially useful promotional tool is trade shows. It's possible through the effective use of displays and exhibits to give the impression of being a more substantial company than you are. Remember, though, that trade shows can get expensive when you figure in travel, exhibit space rental, displays, and the cost of management time spent at the show.

Your business plan should give some indication of the scope of your promotional effort—the publications you plan to target and the kind of material you plan to present. News releases, of course, are basic. Cultivating personal relationships with industry editors is also important.

What about PR firms? It's easy to opt out of the do-it-yourself approach and hire a public relations firm to handle promotional efforts. The only problem with that is it's expensive—typically $3,000 to $4,000 monthly—and the work may not get done as effectively as when the company's officials are actively involved. Press people often prefer to deal directly with company executives rather than with an intermediary like a public relations specialist.

The downside to doing your own PR, of course, is that it takes time and energy that could be devoted to running the business.

Your business plan should specify which promotional approach you'll take, since the decision to go with a professional PR firm will involve planning for the expenditure.

Making your promotion productive. When inquiries come in as a result of publicity, your challenge is to determine not only whether the inquiry is serious, but just how serious. One way to do that is to rate the inquiries on a 1-to-4 scale, as follows:

1. Immediate prospect. Needs product/service yesterday.
2. Near-term prospect.
3. Long-term prospect. We're thinking about committing.
4. Informational prospect. We want the information for our file.

You then plan your most intense follow-up sales efforts for those falling into the first two categories.

4. What Evidence Do You Have of Success?

Your ability to get articles written about your company or by your company's executives imparts an image of success that can be used with brochures and other written material to help close sales. Beyond these tools, though, there's another that is often the most effective—what I refer to as "love letters." Love letters are written compliments from your customers or clients. Whether they're used by your salespeople to impress prospects or in your business plan to impress investors, they can be extremely effective.

I saw one example of a particularly effective use of love letters on Sunset Boulevard in Los Angeles, in the window of a store specializing in custom-made men's shirts. I was drawn to the window because my father was in that business some years back and I had worked in his store.

In the window were the usual displays of freshly pressed dress shirts, along with photos of movie stars. One was of Burt Reynolds, with the inscription, "Thanks always for a perfect fit." Another was of Sylvester Stallone, which said simply, "Brilliance." And a third one was from Kirk Douglas, with a similarly complimentary inscription. Talk about impressive love letters! My father would have killed for those kinds of testimonials.

Love letters don't necessarily fall into your hands, so be prepared to ask customers who you know are satisfied to provide them. Or just ask the customers for comments and take notes so that you can transcribe them into your promotional material.

Another tactic to impress prospects is to use a partial list of customers or clients. This tactic can be tricky, however, because some customers don't take kindly to having their names used, so approach them gingerly about using their names.

Formulating a Sales Program: The Software Publishing Model

Software Publishing's sales outlet is retail stores. The company's executives realized that their most immediate challenge was getting the product sold to retailers (see Exhibit 8–1). For a product priced (to retailers) at between $50 and $100 each and sold in quantities of anywhere from a dozen to several hundred at a time, the best sales outlets were direct mail, mass distributors, and assorted sales reps.

The company had already experimented with advertising. And because it expected venture capital backing, it could plan for additional advertising as well as trade show exhibits.

To support its sales effort, the company planned what it called a "Push" sales program, which was a way to provide demonstration materials to retailers. The company also planned "seminar kits."

As shown in Exhibit 8–1, the company provides data about its promotional effort, customer profile, and number of retailers.

Formulating a Sales Program: The Celestial Seasonings Model

For a company that already has multimillion dollars of revenues, the sales and promotion task becomes at once simpler and more complex, as Celestial Seasonings' business plan illustrates. Business life certainly becomes simpler when your sales channels are well established to outlets like supermarkets. Because Celestial Seasonings had clearly established those outlets, its business plan does not dwell on that fundamental issue.

The complexity comes in having a dozen or so different

products that have achieved varying degrees of success. The appropriate Celestial Seasonings business plan section—identified as a "Marketing Action Plan" but in reality a Sales and Promotion plan—describes the sales and promotional events (see Exhibit 8–2).

Cutting through the lingo and insider shorthand, Celestial Seasonings has come up with a combination of incentives for distributors, support for retailers in the form of displays and free samples, and television advertising. It is also trying to expand its reach to new customers—such as customers of health food stores and in various geographical markets.

The objectives and tactics for reaching the objectives aren't random. Because the company had been in business for several years, the tactics are based on real-life experience, which is always the best kind.

EXERCISES

Worksheets for this chapter are provided on page 222

1. Determine an alternative sales distribution approach to the one you use or are planning to use and document its feasibility for adding to sales.

2. Identify three publications that could publish articles about your company and provide subjects and approaches for getting the articles published.

3. Identify three sources for "love letters" that you can include in your business plan.

EXHIBIT 8-1:

SOFTWARE PUBLISHING CORP.: FORMULATING A SALES PROGRAM

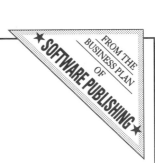

FROM THE BUSINESS PLAN OF ★ SOFTWARE PUBLISHING ★

Channels of Distribution:

SPC products will be sold through retail computer stores. At present there are approximately 1,100 Apple-authorized dealers worldwide. As of 2/1/81 PFS is being carried by 200, or roughly 18%, of these dealers. It is SPC's objective to have its products in at least 50% of these dealers by the end of 1981. To achieve this SPC will be using direct-mail techniques, mass distributors, and independent commissioned sales representatives.

Sales Programs:

SPC has been using a strong advertising program to "Pull" Apple owners and prospective owners into the retail stores. The present PFS ad is being run in 3 Apple owner magazines with a combined circulation of 70,000. These publications are:

> Softalk (30K)
> Nibble (10K)
> Apple Orchard (30K)

SPC plans to expand advertising significantly in the Spring of 1981 to include Business/Professional Publications like *The Wall Street Journal*, plus major computer magazines like *Creative Computing*. SPC will also initiate trade show participation starting in July.

In February of 1981 SPC will begin its first direct-mail campaign by sending the PFS flyer to 2,000 Apple owners in the New York/New Jersey area. This program will be expanded throughout the U.S. after evaluation of the first mailing.

SPC has also launched a "Push" sales program by providing Apple dealers with the PFS flyer for point-of-ad display. We are finding that many dealers use PFS to demonstrate the ease of use and value of an Apple computer, resulting in PFS and Apple sales. SPC will also be providing dealers with seminar kits on using SPC products to increase system sales.

EXHIBIT 8-2:

CELESTIAL SEASONINGS:
STRATEGY FOR A MASS-MARKET PROMOTION

MARKETING ACTION PLAN
SPECIFIC OBJECTIVES AND STRATEGIES

OBJECTIVE

1. Increase gross grocery distribution to 82% ACV and key item distribution as follows:

Sleepytime	75%
Mandarin Orange Spice	75
Country Apple	75
Cinnamon Rose	75
Almond Sunset	60
Red Zinger	60
Sunburst C	40

STRATEGIES

a. Implement 3 major trade promotional events

- Fall   Open Stock/Display Promotion
  - runs in October for both distributors and direct
  - all direct open stock items on deal
  - distributor items on deal: ST, MOS, CA, CR
  - 13M displays with ST, MOS, CA, CR
  - 72 free packettes with each display (exceptions where market conditions dictate)
  - distributor - 10% off on O/S and display; $5 spiff per display to selected accounts
  - direct - 1.44 of invoice on O/S; 11% off invoice + 4% early buy on displays
  - merchandise incentive program for distributors and selected direct customers

- Winter   Open Stock/Display Promotion
  - runs in January for direct, February for distributors
  - all direct open stock items on deal
  - distributor items on deal: ST, MOS, AS, SC

- 8M displays with ST, MOS, AS, SC
- allowances, packettes, incentives identical to Fall Promotion

- Spring Direct Promotion
  - runs in April for direct only
  - all direct open stock items on deal
  - 1.44 off invoice

b. Implement trade promotion on key item(s) needing major distribution push

- Sunburst C
  - September prefall promotion
  - 20% direct allowance; 10% distribution allowance

c. Heavy-Up direct markets with regionally allocated consumer advertising and promotion funds

- Freestanding Inserts.
  - scheduled for November, February, and April in support of trade promotion events
  - 47 million combined circulation (+25% vs. F'83)
  - 2/5 page ad with 15cts coupon (or 3/5 page with 15cts coupon and premium offer)
- Regional Print Advertising
  - *New York Times Magazine* supporting New York City market
  - *Sunset* Magazine supporting west coast markets
- Spot Television
  - Boston and Philadelphia in 2-week flights supporting key trade promotional events (November and February)

d. Provide grocery trade media funds to increase buyer awareness and reasons for stocking.

- *Progressive Grocer* July and October issues

OBJECTIVE

2. Expand awareness of Celestial Seasonings to 40% of U.S. households from 35%.

   STRATEGIES

   a. Continue to build on "Soothing Teas" positioning across all elements of plan.
      - Include in all advertising and promotional materials; execute on all IMA packages.

   b. Focus majority of working A&M dollars into advertising.

   c. Continue to focus the majority of advertising funds against the general consumer.
      - General consumer advertising programs
        - 35 total pages in eleven national magazines
        - spot television for 4 weeks in Boston and Philadelphia at 175 GRP's per week
        - General consumer target national (women 25-49)

   d. Continue the test of television in 4 cities; expand use of TV if positive results are seen.
      - TV markets are San Diego, Sacramento, Salt Lake City, Boise
      - Media flight to begin in January for 6 weeks
      - General consumer target in test cities

OBJECTIVE

3. Expand trial of Celestial Seasonings to 23% of U.S. households from 20%

   STRATEGIES

   a. Introduce Food service line in 2nd quarter
      - 7 items in line: ST, MOS, CA, CR, AS, SC, Assorted Pack
      - November/December introduction
      - 15% billback introductory allowance
      - accrual fund program to gain promotions in distributor price book flyers & mailers, 3–5% paid quarterly
      - co-op advertising allowance for end-users; menu cards; table tents

b. Increase distribution of Variety Pack 4 to 50% ACV
- September promotion on VP-4
- 20% allowance direct to gain authorization and placement; 10% allowance distributor

c. Double the number of trial devices used by consumers
- Freestanding insert 15cts coupons (47 million circulation)
- Tie-in with Nabisco Toasted Wheat & Raisins cereal; 15cts coupon on package back; supported by advertising and point-of-sale (5MM circulation)
- Packettes on displays (1MM delivered)
- Food service samples (5MM delivered)
- Magazine ad with sample and coupon test (500M circulation)

d. Overlay extra funds in geographical opportunity markets (high CDI, low share)
- Freestanding inserts, as outlined above
- Spot television and regional print, as outlined above

e. Test potential of single-serving food service product as trial-generating device
- Magazine ad with sample and coupon; test area circulation 500M
- Development of promotional package and literature for distribution in medical offices

OBJECTIVE
4. Improve relative product quality index by 15%.

STRATEGIES

a. Improve at least 4 of the top 7 brands' plus Lemon Mist through flavor improvement

b. Identify greatest areas for RPQ improvement in packaging modifications

OBJECTIVE

5. Strengthen health food store franchise.

STRATEGIES

a. Provide continuity of trade promotions through the year to health food distributors
- Health Food Tea of the Month
  - January: Emperor's Choice (10% off)
  - March: Chamomile, Grandma's Tummy Mint (10% off)

b. Maintain advertising pressure against the Health Food consumer through shift in advertising funds balance to lower CPM, broader reach books
- 25 total advertising pages in 6 magazines
- 14.4M circulation (+9% versus F'83 on -5% budget)

c. Implement continuity consumer promotions to encourage greater purchase frequency among loyal consumers
- Fall premium offer: 1984 Celestial Seasonings calendar. Promoted with in-back cards and point-of-sale materials
- Winter premium offer: to be determined
- Recipes using Celestial Seasonings products; promoted with in-pack cards

d. Provide continuity health trade advertising
- Health trade advertising program
  - 25 total pages in three trade magazines
  - heavy up schedule in September and October with two ads in two books each month

e. Improve quality and timeliness of Whistlestop
- New, improved 4-color masthead
- Develop editorial schedule maximizing business opportunities
- Inclusion of contemporary, useful advice for retail managers
- Improve writing style and retailer comprehension by using experienced newsletter writer

OBJECTIVE

6. Build pound share in New York City to a 37% minimum; Philadelphia to 37%; Chicago to 32%.

   STRATEGIES

   a. Convert NYC to direct sales basis by 8/1/83

   b. Provide heavy-up advertising support
   - Overlay TV support in all 3 markets around each FSI drop
   - *New York Times Magazine*-4 pages, including September Home Entertainment Issue

   c. Provide FSI coupon support, NYC for the first time
   - January and April FSI's include New York City for the first time

   d. Overlay magazine sampling program in NYC and Chicago metro areas (February edition of *Woman's Day*).

   e. Establish Kosher certification
   - certification to be established during 1st quarter
   - mailing announcement to Jewish community during 2nd quarter

OBJECTIVE

7. Evaluate and begin development of promising new tea concept(s)

   STRATEGIES

   a. Establish criteria for evaluation of new concepts
   b. Generate new tea concepts by 7/83
   c. Test and evaluate concepts by 10/83

PRICING OBJECTIVE

PRICING

The pricing objective is to maintain/lower retail prices while minimizing gross margin erosion.

   Strategies

   a. Take no price increase
   b. Raise net selling price and affect lower shelf prices through direct account conversions in all regions but the Southeast U. S.

Financial Issues: How Are You Doing?

F INANCIAL ISSUES tend to be unpopular among entrepreneurs. Some find the subject tedious. Others find it intimidating. The result is that many entrepreneurs do nothing. Finances in many businesses become the state of the checkbook each morning. If there's cash, the business is still around and if there's no cash, the business has major problems.

One of the major benefits of creating a business plan is that it forces entrepreneurs to confront their company's finances squarely. That's because a business plan isn't complete until entrepreneurs can demonstrate that all the wonderful plans concerning strategy, markets, products, and sales will actually come together to create a business that will be self-sustaining over the short term and profitable over the long term.

Note that the financial section of the business plan is done last, after you've had a chance to make your marketing, production, and selling plans. Here is where you attach precise dollar figures to those plans and determine how those figures add up in the context of several different financial statements.

The financial section of the business plan should consist of

three types of standard financial statements:
1. Cash flow statement
2. Income statement (sometimes referred to as profit/loss statement)
3. Balance sheet

Before discussing these statements in more detail, a few points need to be made about financial statements in general.

• **Make them conventional.** It's one thing to be creative in analyzing the market or coming up with sales approaches, but the financial statements should be done according to what financial types refer to as "generally accepted accounting principles." Bankers and investors examine dozens of financial statements every day and are accustomed to seeing expenses, margins, taxes, and other items identified in their customary ways and in their customary order. The tried-and-true not only makes them feel comfortable but also enables them to review the financial state of the company quickly and easily. If they see financial statements at odds with what's customary, they are likely to be skeptical about the expertise of the entrepreneurs and the state of the business, which is not a good way to win friends and influence people.

Sophisticated investors who become interested in your business will use your financial projections to calculate the potential future value of the company. Companies tend to be valued on the basis of some combination and/or multiple of sales, profits, and asset value. Investors who are confident in the numbers they see in the financial projections will attempt to calculate a company's value in the future to determine what an investment today might lead to. If they're convinced they can get the appreciation they want, they may invest.

• **Cover the past and the future.** Generally speaking, the business plan should provide detailed financial results for the previous three years. It should use those results to develop projected financial statements for the upcoming three to five years—as I've mentioned earlier, there must be a connection between what happened in the past and what you project for the future. If sales have been rising at 10% annually for the previous three years, you can't project them to rise at 50% annually for the upcoming three years without some fairly compelling reasons.

One obvious question concerns how to handle the start-up company, which has no previous financial history. Start-up entrepreneurs can make only financial projections, which they must be able to justify. Bankers and investors ordinarily assume that a start-up company's projections are wildly optimistic; the standard preamble that your numbers are "conservative" doesn't go far enough in providing reassurance. Ideally, you've done some test marketing and/or have hard experience with a comparable business to provide some basis for your projections.

• **Explain your assumptions.** At some point in the financial section of your business plan you need to explain the assumptions that underlie your projections. That is, how did you arrive at your estimate of general and administrative expenses? Have you worked out a commission structure with your sales reps or are you just estimating the sales costs? And how much of your sales increases come from expanding volume and how much from price increases?

• **Consider several scenarios.** One way to ease the concerns of outsiders worried about your projections being overly optimistic is to provide several potential outcomes. The first would be your expected projections; the second, a "worst-case" scenario—if there's an industry recession, here's how your financial situation would be affected. Third, you may want to include a "best-case" scenario—how things would work if everything went your way. The best-case numbers may look impressive, but they won't carry much weight with experienced investors.

• **Avoid "spreadsheetitis."** In this day and age of easy-to-use computer spreadsheet programs (e.g., Lotus, Excel), the task of putting together financial projections is much less time consuming than it was in the days of adding machines. As a result, it's possible to assemble financial statements that go into excruciating detail—more than what bankers or investors want to see and more than what is truly necessary. Some professional investors refer to the page upon page of financial statements that weigh down some business plans as "spreadsheetitis."

One venture capitalist told me of a technique he uses with entrepreneurs who present what he considers to be excessive tabulations. "How did you come up with line 18 on page 24?" he asks. "The computer came up with that," is the typical response. To which the venture capitalist responds, "Is the computer going to be running the business?"

Just as the prose should be concise and to the point, so should the financial statements.

• **Consult an accountant.** All smaller companies should have an accountant involved at least in tax preparation. Ask this accountant, or another accountant with whom you may have a relationship, to review your financial statements. Indeed, if you consult your accountant for business advice, you may want to get him or her involved in the financial planning process early.

Parts of the financial statements, particularly the balance sheet, can involve technical issues such as how assets and liabilities should be classified. Moreover, an accountant can help you assess how a banker might view your financial statements.

Bankers tend to use ratios from the balance sheet—such as assets to liabilities and debt to equity—in assessing the creditworthiness of businesses. The ratios they consider satisfactory can vary from industry to industry. If your ratios are out of line with the bankers' viewpoint, an accountant can suggest steps you can take to adjust these ratios.

Financial Issues: How Are You Doing?

147

The remainder of this chapter provides explanations of the three types of financial statements, with special emphasis on the cash flow statement because it is the basis of the other two.

Cash Flow: The Business Lifeline

All business owners know what cash flow is—if not technically, then emotionally. Nevertheless, it's worthwhile to approach this subject from the very beginning because it is key to business success. Some business school professors have even begun to impart to their students the latest thinking about cash flow: "Cash flow is more important than your mother."

A useful way to think about cash flow is to view the business as a living organism. Cash is the nutrient that runs through its arteries and veins. The brain might be viewed as the product or service, the heart as the marketing, and the stomach as the finances, at which point it all begins to get a little messy. If you don't have enough cash flow, though, rest assured that the living organism turns into a skeleton.

The essential point about cash flow that is often overlooked is that it is different from profit and, for a growing business, much more important. It's possible to run out of cash and go broke even if you have a lot of purchase orders because you aren't being paid in a timely way.

This is a problem that has afflicted more than one *Inc.* 500 company. One such company that sold a big-ticket item (a computer software product for $50,000 and up) was caught in that bind as its sales climbed from $2 million to $5 million. The orders were there, but the cash came in as late as six months after a salesperson received a commitment to buy. That's because the corporate purchase orders might take another two or three months to be executed and the bills another one to three months to be paid after that. This company's executives had to skip a few paydays, negotiate with suppliers to keep essential products and services coming, and otherwise struggle to stay afloat until the cash came in. Things were so tight that the company's treasurer found himself monitoring cash flow on a daily basis.

Cash flow can also be used as a planning tool. By monitoring cash flow on a regular basis as cash comes in and goes out, you'll see a pattern that enables you to plan for the future.

This becomes very important, especially if you want to expand or go after new markets. You can quickly calculate the effect of such actions on cash flow and determine whether you'll need to seek a bank loan or other financing or whether you can support the new activity from internally generated funds.

Calculating cash flow. Quite simply, cash flow is a record of cash available at different points in times. It's usually monitored on a monthly basis. A cash flow statement seems complicated at first glance, but it's really very simple, and it's extremely important as a planning tool.

Exhibit 9–1 provides a standard cash flow statement. You begin with the cash on hand at the beginning of the month. Then you add the receipts during the month—from customers, royalties, commissions, interest, and so forth.

From that, you subtract the actual disbursements—the cash going out each month in the form of fixed and variable expenses. Fixed expenses are such things as rent, debt, salaries—items you're committed to for the long term and can't easily change. Variable expenses include advertising, office supplies, promotion, consulting, and other such expenses that can be easily increased or decreased from month to month.

The result is the amount of cash available at the end of the month. The cash flow is the difference between what you started with and ended with.

Assembling a cash flow statement: chronicling the past. To help you get started in putting together your own cash flow statement, this section describes the cash flow statement of a hypothetical architectural firm, ABC Architectural Services.

149

The cash flow statement is for the four months just ended (see Exhibit 9–2). (For the purpose of the exercise, we assume that we're now at April 30.)

A few notes about this company:

It employed seven people in January and received two new architectural design contracts in January for $25,000 each. These jobs should each take five months to complete and are payable as completed.

ABC Architectural Services added two employees at $36,000 per year in February and one employee at $24,000 in March to help on the new contracts. It added 50% more space in April. And aside from the two new contracts, business is assumed to remain level.

Now let's see what the cash flow statement tells us. First, we see that the expenses associated with direct materials and equipment move upward. That's because those new employees will require office supplies, like drafting materials, desks, lamps, wall dividers, maybe a computer terminal and some software. Next, the main fixed expense, which is salaries, goes up substantially in February and March.

The other side of the cash flow equation is the incoming cash—in this business and most others a function of the collection of receivables. At ABC Architectural Services, the new employees will require some training and assistance during their first month on the job, so the assumption is that it will take them two months—February and March—to do the first month's work. Even so, the assumption is that the company collects for that entire first month of work during the month of April, so in April there's a $10,000 jump.

The impact of the outflow and inflow just described is apparent in the cash balances. ABC Architectural Services begins with $55,000 cash on January 1, as shown in the upper left-hand corner, and by April 30 it's down to $12,000, as shown in the lower right-hand corner. Clearly, its position is less comfortable.

An important point becomes apparent. The expenses pile up

a lot faster than the revenues come in. Just because a company gets two $25,000 contracts doesn't mean it suddenly has $50,000.

This company placed itself in a precarious financial position because it didn't structure its contracts to allow for its small size and vulnerable cash position. If those two new clients had taken 90 days to make their first payments instead of 30 days, at the end of April the company would have been down to $2,000 cash. By May, it could have been out of business.

Assembling a cash flow statement—projecting the future. The previous section used actual financial results to gain insights into business strengths and weaknesses. But it's possible to take those results and look into the future by doing financial projections.

Exhibit 9–3 is a projection for the next four months for ABC Architectural Services. The managers of the firm realized cash was diminishing, so they decided they had to hold the line on expenses; thus, the material expenses level off and the equipment expenses decline.

But because they've added 50% more space earlier in the year, they feel an obligation to make that space as attractive as possible. I would argue that these expenses, particularly materials, are probably too high. Unfortunately, they're stuck with the salaries they brought in, unless they want to take the drastic step of laying off the new employees.

Next, the executives resolve to watch the receivables very closely, to ensure that enough cash is coming in. This is reflected in the projected collection of receivables, which continues to rise.

The effects of the planning and projections can be seen in the company's cash position. It continues downward for May and into June, but by the end of June and July it is heading back up and, by August, it's gotten a good deal healthier.

Monitoring the cash flow in this way should make it apparent to ABC Architectural Services' executives that they need to make some adjustments—in their approaches to billing and to hiring. On the billing front, for instance, the owners will likely want to negotiate fixed-fee/monthly installment contracts or regular billing with a substantial upfront payment.

If this cash flow projection were continued, another problem would become apparent: what is this company going to do to keep the three new employees busy after July when the two contracts have been completed?

The Income Statement: The Bottom Line

The income statement is the one we all tend to focus our attention on because it provides the proverbial "bottom line"—the company's profit or loss. It's usually done on a quarterly basis.

As you look at the basic income statement shown in Exhibit 9–4, you'll notice that it seems a lot like the cash flow statement. You start with your revenues less commissions. From that, you subtract direct labor (drafters and architects, for instance, for an architectural firm) and materials.

The result is a subtotal that gives you your gross profit or loss. (The percentage of gross profit to revenues can be a very useful number. It's your gross margin and can help you compare yourself with others in your industry—it tells you immediately whether your labor or other costs are way out of line.)

From your gross profit, you subtract indirect labor (nonbillable time, for instance), administrative labor, and expenses (general and administrative), along with any depreciation. The result is another subtotal that is your pretax net profit or loss.

From that, you subtract a provision for taxes, and the result, at long last, is your net income, or the net increase (or decrease) in retained earnings.

Once again, keep in mind that for smaller businesses, the income statement is less important than the cash flow statement, since it's possible for a business to run out of cash early in a quarter, even though it's heading toward profits at the end of the quarter. The primary difference between the cash flow and income statements, then, is timing.

The Balance Sheet: A Statement of Business Health

The balance sheet is more esoteric. It shows the state of the company's assets and liabilities at a particular point in time. As a statement of the company's resources, it is important in determining basic business health (see sample in Exhibit 9–5).

On one side of the balance sheet are the company's assets—current assets such as cash and accounts receivable and fixed assets like furniture and computers.

On the other side of the balance sheet (the bottom half of the exhibit) are the liabilities—the current liabilities like accounts payable and notes payable and long-term liabilities such as equity.

The assets and liabilities must add up to the same number and be balanced. That's why it's called the balance sheet.

Balance sheets are very useful for measuring the health of manufacturing, wholesaling, and other product-oriented businesses in which assets can be measured in terms of equipment and inventory. The balance sheet is less useful for evaluating service businesses. Indeed, the balance sheet can be misleading for an architectural or personnel placement business since their primary assets are their people.

Unfortunately, bankers tend to rely heavily on the balance sheet, using ratios of various assets and liabilities. As the economy becomes service oriented, however, bankers are gradually changing their attitudes, so it pays to shop around if you encounter resistance from some bankers.

Projecting A New Airline's Finances: The People Express Model

An excellent example of assumptions underlying a business plan is provided in the People Express financials (see Exhibit 9–6). Here we find a list of 12 assumptions that help clarify the projections that follow. Most have to do with revenues and expenses associated with flying the company's expected three-plane fleet. Thus, we learn in points 7, 8, and 9 that revenues don't include certain items that could become important later, like excess baggage and charter fees. And we learn in points 4 and 5 how the aircraft lease and personnel costs are figured in.

Following the stated assumptions, the plan provides further detail in table form about what it calls its "Preliminary Operating Plan" (see Exhibit 9–6a). The reader learns what expectations are about the number of miles flown each month, the number of passengers to be carried, and so on. Someone familiar with the airline industry can easily determine how realistic the assumptions are and thereby decide whether or not to invest or become a supplier or otherwise become involved.

Next comes the company's cash flow statement, which is labeled "Preliminary Statement of Results" (see Exhibit 9–6b). It becomes apparent that the statement is done on a monthly basis, which is appropriate for a start-up company. Because cash flow is so important, it's necessary to project on a monthly basis for at least the first year; some would suggest it should be shown monthly for three years and thereafter on a quarterly basis.

An interesting twist in the People Express cash flow statement is the incorporation of expected financing. The bottom of the statement shows the effect of $6 million of investment funds on the company's cash flow. This is usually preferable to showing results without investment or loan funds, leading to negative cash flow.

Conclusion

As should be clear by now, financial statements serve a much larger purpose than impressing bankers or venture capitalists. They are an important monitoring and planning tool. Almost like an X-ray or EKG enables a doctor to get an important view of a patient's condition, so a cash flow or income statement provides special insights into a business's condition. And even more than a crystal ball or palm-reading, these statements provide a basis for projecting into the future. The more history that exists, the more accurate the projections are likely to be. Indeed, it's even possible to take components of the cash flow results—promotion or direct labor, for instance—and track them separately to determine correlations with overall cash flow or profits.

Finance may not be your favorite subject, but it should rank among your highest priorities.

EXERCISES

Worksheets for this chapter are provided on page 224

1. Here is important financial data necessary to construct a cash flow statement for the ABC Personnel Agency:

January 1, cash on hand was $48,000.
Income from client billings was as follows:
January: $36,000
February: $30,000
March: $28,000
April: $28,000
Expenditures for the company, $496,500/year, as follows:
Annual Salaries (including fringe benefits):
President: $100,000
Senior Vice-President: $70,000
Vice-President: $48,000
Office Manager: $42,000
2 Placement Counselors: $36,000
2 Associate Placement Counselors: $30,000
2 Trainees: $24,000
2 Secretaries: $20,000
Other expenses:
Rent: $52,000
Utilities: $6,000
Phone: $6,000
Professional services (accounting, legal): $15,000
Sales expenses (travel and entertainment): $24,000
Supplies and forms: $12,000
Furniture and equipment: $6,000
Bank debt service (11% on $50,000 credit line): $5,500

2. Construct a cash flow statement for the ABC Personnel Agency for the first four months of the year.

- What is the trend of the cash flow over this period?
- Does this trend present any potential problem? If so what steps might the company take to correct the situation?

(After working out a statement, compare your results with those in Exercise 9–A.)

EXERCISE 9-A:

ABC PERSONNEL SERVICES
MONTHLY CASH FLOW STATEMENT

ABC PERSONNEL SERVICES				
MONTHLY CASH FLOW STATEMENT ($000)				
MONTH	Jan.	Feb.	March	April
ITEM				
BEGINNING CASH BALANCE	48.0	42.63	31.26	17.89
RECEIPTS				
Collection of receivables	36.0	30.0	28.0	28.0
Interest income				
Other				
TOTAL RECEIPTS	36.0	30.0	28.0	28.0
CASH DISBURSEMENTS				
Accounts payable				
Supplies	1.0	1.0	1.0	1.0
Direct labor				
Equipment	0.5	0.5	0.5	0.5
Salaries	30.83	30.83	30.83	30.83
Rent	4.33	4.33	4.33	4.33
Phone	0.5	0.5	0.5	0.5
Utilities	0.5	0.5	0.5	0.5
Insurance				
Sales expenses	2.0	2.0	2.0	2.0
Taxes				
Loan payments	0.46	0.46	0.46	0.46
Prof. services	1.25	1.25	1.25	1.25
TOTAL DISBURSEMENTS	41.37	41.37	41.37	41.37
TOTAL CASH FLOW	−5.37	−11.37	−13.37	−13.37
ENDING CASH BALANCE	42.63	31.26	17.89	4.52

EXHIBIT 9-1:

STANDARD CASH FLOW STATEMENT

COMPANY NAME				
PRO-FORMA MONTHLY CASH FLOW STATEMENT 199__ – 199__ ($000)				
MONTH				
ITEM				
BEGINNING CASH BALANCE				
RECEIPTS				
Collection of receivables				
Interest income				
Other				
TOTAL RECEIPTS				
CASH DISBURSEMENTS				
Accounts payable				
Supplies				
Direct labor				
Equipment				
Salaries				
Rent				
Insurance				
Advertising				
Taxes				
Loan payments				
Other				
TOTAL DISBURSEMENTS				
TOTAL CASH FLOW				
ENDING CASH BALANCE				

EXHIBIT 9-2:

ABC ARCHITECTURAL SERVICES:
MONTHLY CASH FLOW STATEMENT, JANUARY–APRIL

ABC ARCHITECTURAL SERVICES				
MONTHLY CASH FLOW STATEMENT ($000)				
ITEM	Jan.	Feb.	March	April
BEGINNING CASH BALANCE	55.0	51.0	38.0	21.0
RECEIPTS				
Collection of receivables	30.0	30.0	30.0	40.0
Interest income	1.0	1.0	1.0	1.0
Other				
TOTAL RECEIPTS	31.0	31.0	31.0	41.0
CASH DISBURSEMENTS				
Accounts payable	3.0	3.0	3.0	3.0
Direct materials	3.0	4.0	4.0	5.0
Direct labor	4.0	4.0	4.0	4.0
Equipment		1.0	2.0	3.0
Salaries	21.0	27.0	29.0	29.0
Rent	2.0	2.0	3.0	3.0
Insurance	0.5	0.5	0.5	0.5
Advertising	0.5	1.0	1.0	1.0
Taxes	1.0	1.5	1.5	1.5
Loan payments				
Other				
TOTAL DISBURSEMENTS	35.0	44.0	48.0	50.0
TOTAL CASH FLOW	–4.0	–13.0	–17.0	–9.0
ENDING CASH BALANCE	51.0	38.0	21.0	12.0

EXHIBIT 9-3:

ABC ARCHITECTURAL SERVICES:
MONTHLY CASH FLOW PROJECTIONS, MAY–JUNE

ABC ARCHITECTURAL SERVICES				
MONTHLY CASH FLOW STATEMENT ($000)				
ITEM	May	June	July	August
BEGINNING CASH BALANCE	12.0	8.0	12.0	24.0
RECEIPTS				
Collection of receivables	50.0	60.0	70.0	80.0
Interest income	1.0	1.0	1.0	1.0
Other				
TOTAL RECEIPTS	51.0	61.0	71.0	81.0
CASH DISBURSEMENTS				
Accounts payable	5.0	7.0	9.0	11.0
Direct materials	8.0	8.0	9.0	9.0
Direct labor	6.0	6.0	6.0	6.0
Equipment	2.0	2.0	1.0	1.0
Salaries	29.0	29.0	29.0	29.0
Rent	3.0	3.0	3.0	3.0
Insurance	0.5	0.5	0.5	0.5
Advertising	0.5	0.5	0.5	0.5
Taxes	1.0	1.0	1.0	1.0
Loan payments				
Other				
TOTAL DISBURSEMENTS	55.0	57.0	59.0	61.0
TOTAL CASH FLOW	−4.0	4.0	12.0	20.0
ENDING CASH BALANCE	8.0	12.0	24.0	44.0

EXHIBIT 9–4:

STANDARD QUARTERLY INCOME STATEMENT

COMPANY NAME				
PRO-FORMA QUARTERLY INCOME STATEMENT 199__ ($000)				
QUARTER				
ITEM				
SALES REVENUES				
Sales commissions				
NET REVENUES				
COST OF GOODS SOLD				
Direct labor				
Materials				
TOTAL				
GROSS MARGIN				
OPERATING EXPENSES				
Selling				
Salaries				
Advertising				
Other				
General-administrative				
Depreciation				
TOTAL				
INCOME (LOSS) FROM OPERATIONS				
INTEREST INCOME (EXPENSE)				
NET INCOME (LOSS)				
PROVISION FOR TAXES				
NET INCOME AFTER TAXES				
NET INCREASE (DECREASE) TO RETAINED EARNINGS				

EXHIBIT 9-5:

STANDARD BALANCE SHEET

COMPANY NAME				
PRO-FORMA QUARTERLY BALANCE SHEET 199__ ($000)				
QUARTER				
ASSETS				
CURRENT ASSETS				
Cash				
Accounts receivable				
Prepaid expenses				
Other				
TOTAL CURRENT ASSETS				
FIXED ASSETS				
Furniture				
Computers				
Equipment				
TOTAL FIXED ASSETS				
TOTAL ASSETS				
LIABILITIES				
CURRENT LIABILITIES				
Accounts payable				
Notes payable				
Taxes payable				
LONG-TERM LIABILITIES				
Equity				
Withdrawals				
NET EQUITY				
TOTAL LIABILITIES AND EQUITY				

EXHIBIT 9-6:

PEOPLE EXPRESS:
FORECAST ASSUMPTIONS

The key assumptions underlying the forecast contained in Exhibits I-III are listed below:

(1)   Each month is assumed to be a 30-day month with no consideration given to holi-
        days or weekends. This results in a 360-day year for operating statistics purposes.
        This 360-day year, in effect, obviates the need to impute a performance factor
        (noncompletion due to weather/mechanical) thus the completion factor ends up at
        about 98.5%.

(2)   The $3,000,000 in preoperating expenses is assumed to be amortized over a five-
        year period on a straight-line basis. ($50,000 per month)

(3)   Expenses incurred in initiating new routes are amortized over the first three months
        of operation in equal parts.

(4)   Aircraft are assumed to be configured with 120 seats. Lease rates are assumed to be
        $105,00 per month per aircraft while the necessary spare parts are assumed to be
        leased at $12,000 per month. The stock of spares increases proportionally with the
        number of aircraft.

(5)   Two-engine aircraft with 2 pilots and 3 cabin personnel are assumed. Aircraft will
        be of the 737-200 or DC-9-30 type. Aircraft are assumed to be utilized 10 hours
        per day with an average flight stage of one hour. The average aircraft speed is 300
        miles per hour.

(6)   Fuel is assumed at $1.00 per gallon. Aircraft of this type will consume 800–850
        gallons per hour depending on conditions.

(7)   Only revenues from passengers are assumed. No beverage/meal revenue, over-the-
        counter freight, excess baggage, mail or other revenue is included in the analyses.

PEOPLE EXPRESS: FORECAST ASSUMPTIONS
continued

(8) Only point-to-point traffic is included. E.g., only traffic from A to B or B to C is included. No traffic or revenue is included for "Bridge" traffic such as A to C.

(9) No costs or revenues are assumed for character or extra-utilization work.

(10) Fare structure assumed is $39 peak and $25 off-peak. About one-third of traffic is assumed to travel at the off-peak fare while approximately two-thirds of the traffic will travel at $39.

(11) No general inflation factor has been assumed for costs or revenues.

(12) The effective balance sheet debt covered by leases is the estimated purchase price of $7,000,000 times the number of aircraft with associated spares leased at any point in time.

EXHIBIT 9-6a:

PEOPLE EXPRESS: PRELIMINARY OPERATING PLAN
JUNE 1981–MAY 1983

	1981							1982					YEAR
1981	JUN	JUL	AUG	SEP	OCT	NOV	DEC	JAN	FEB	MAR	APR	MAY	
Number of Aircraft	3	3	3	3	3	4	5	5	5	5	6	6	
OPERATING STATISTICS													
Fleet Hours Operated	900	900	900	900	900	1,200	1,500	1,500	1,500	1,500	1,800	1,800	15,300
Plane Miles (000)	270	270	270	270	270	360	450	450	450	450	5,40	5,40	4,590
Available Seat Miles (000)	32,400	32,400	32,400	32,400	32,400	43,200	54,000	54,000	54,000	54,000	64,800	64,800	550,800
Trips Flown	900	900	900	900	900	1,200	1,500	1,500	1,500	1,500	1,800	1,800	15,300
TRAFFIC STATISTICS													
Passengers Carried Per Trip	50	59	65	56	63	62	67	60	60	62	57	59	60
Passenger Load Factor (%)	41.6	49.2	54.2	46.7	52.5	51.7	55.8	50	50	51.7	47.5	49.2	50.0083
Passengers Boarded	45,000	53,100	58,500	50,400	56700	74,400	100,500	90,000	90,000	93,000	102600	106,200	920,400
Rev Passngr Mi Flown (000)	13,500	15,900	17,550	15,120	17,010	22,320	30,150	27,000	27,000	27,900	30780	31,860	276,090
REVENUES (000)	$1,575	$1,859	$2,048	$1,764	$1,985	$2,604	$3,518	$3,150	$3,150	$3,255	$3,591	$3,717	$32,216

Financial Issues:
How Are
You Doing?

9

People Express: Preliminary Operating Plan
continued

1982	1982 JUN	JUL	AUG	SEP	OCT	NOV	DEC	1983 JAN	FEB	MAR	APR	MAY	YEAR
Number of Aircraft	8	8	8	8	8	9	10	10	10	10	10	10	
OPERATING STATISTICS													
Fleet Hours Operated	2,400	2,400	2,400	2,400	2,400	2,700	3,000	3,000	3,000	3,000	3,000	3,000	32,700
Plane Miles (000)	720	720	720	720	720	810	900	900	900	900	900	900	9810
Available Seat Miles	86,400	86,400	86,400	86,400	86,400	97,200	108,000	108,000	108,000	108,000	108,000	108,000	1,177,200
Trips Flown	2,400	2,400	2,400	2,400	2,400	2,700	3,000	3000	3,000	3,000	3,000	3,000	32,700
TRAFFIC STATISTICS													
Passengers Carried Per Trip	65	69	72	60	66	62	68	63	63	64	65	65	65.1667
Passenger Load Factor (%)	54.2	57.5	60	50	55	51.7	56.7	52.5	52.5	53.3	54.2	54.2	54.3167
Passengers Boarded	156,000	165,600	172,800	144,000	158,400	167,400	204,000	189,000	189,000	192,000	195,000	195,000	2,128,200
Rev Passngr Mi Flown (000)	46,800	49,680	51,840	43,200	47,520	50,220	61,200	56,700	56,700	57,600	58,500	58,500	638,460
REVENUES (000)	**$5,460**	**$5,796**	**$6,048**	**$5,040**	**$5,544**	**$5,859**	**$7,140**	**$6,615**	**$6,615**	**$6,720**	**$6,825**	**$6,825**	**$74,487**

EXHIBIT 9-6b:

PEOPLE EXPRESS: PRELIMINARY STATEMENT OF RESULTS: JUNE 1981–MAY 1982

(000)	1981 JUN	JUL	AUG	SEP	OCT	NOV	DEC	1982 JAN	FEB	MAR	APR	MAY	YEAR
INCOME STATEMENT													
Passenger Revenue	$1,575	$1,859	$2,048	$1,764	$1,985	$2,604	$3,518	$3,150	$3,150	$3,255	$3,591	$3,717	$32,216
Expenses													
Aircraft/Spares Lease Cost	$351	$351	$351	$351	$351	$468	$585	$585	$585	$585	$702	$702	$5,967
Amortiz Pre-Oper Exp	$50	$50	$50	$50	$50	$50	$50	$50	$50	$50	$50	$50	$600
Amortiz Exp Assoc w/Added Rtes						$140	$140	$140			$90	$90	$600
Operating Expense	$1,449	$1,449	$1,449	$1,449	$1,449	$1,932	$2,415	$2,415	$2,415	$2,415	$2,898	$2,898	$24,633
Total Expense	$1,850	$1,850	$1,850	$1,850	$1,850	$2,590	$3,190	$3,190	$3,050	$3,050	$3,740	$3,740	$31,800
Profit/loss (Pre-Tax)	($275)	$9	$198	($86)	$135	$14	$328	($40)	$100	$205	($149)	($23)	$416
SOURCES AND USES OF FUNDS													
Sources													
Equity Financing	$6,000												$6,000
Cash Results of Opers	($225)	$59	$248	($36)	$185	$204	$518	$150	$150	$255	($9)	$117	$1,616
Total Sources	$5,775	$59	$248	($36)	$185	$204	$518	$150	$150	$255	($9)	$117	$7,616
Uses													
Pre-Oper Expenses	$3,000												$3,000
Lease Deposits	$225					$300					$75		$600
Added Route Expenses						$420					$270		$690
Total Uses	$3,225					$720					$345		$4,290
BEGINNING CASH BALANCE	$6,000	$2,550	$2,609	$2,857	$2,821	$3,006	$2,490	$3,008	$3,158	$3,308	$3,563	$3,209	$6,000
ENDING CASH BALANCE	$2,550	$2,609	$2,857	$2,821	$3,006	$2,490	$3,008	$3,158	$3,308	$3,563	$3,209	$3,326	$3,326

PART THREE:

COMPLETING
THE PLAN

Tailoring the Plan

ANAGERS OF small businesses in some Mediterranean and European countries have long been known to keep three sets of accounting records.

One set, presenting a dismal picture of the business, is for the government and its tax collectors. Another set, presenting a rosier side (but not too rosy), is for the absentee owners. And a third set—the real results with all the profits spelled out—is for the manager.

The point for business owners writing a business plan isn't that you should doctor the records, but rather that you shouldn't feel locked into writing the business plan for your company. With word processing as sophisticated as it is, there's nothing that says you can't have two, three, or more versions of a business plan.

Moreover, it's essential to remember the point made in Chapter 1—the business plan is a selling document. It must sell your business to constituencies important to your business. The goal in this chapter is to identify those constituencies and determine what they are seeking.

**The Customized
Business Plan**

It might seem as if I'm complicating matters by suddenly suggesting the possibility of writing several business plans. After all, you might ask, if I'm having difficulty writing one business plan, won't I simply compound my problems by trying to write two or more plans?

My experience is that you will actually find it easier to address the plan to specific audiences rather than to an abstract, all-inclusive, single audience. When you know your audience, you can "speak" to those readers in terms you know they want to hear or do not want to hear.

Here's an example. I was involved in helping prepare a business plan for a 12-year-old electronics company with about $10 million in annual sales. Three years of declining profits had spurred the four principal owners to write a business plan. They felt that their managers needed the structure and discipline of a written plan to solve some chronic problems and turn the company around.

The owners, who were in their late forties and early fifties, also felt that putting together a written plan would help them set some realistic goals for themselves. When they started discussing this part of the planning process, they concluded that what they really wanted to accomplish over the next five years was to get the company profitable again so that it could be sold and they could exit to early retirement.

Not surprisingly, the owners didn't want to share with their managers and employees who would see the plan the objective to sell the business, for fear of alarming them about something that wouldn't necessarily affect them adversely. So the owners created two business plans.

One plan was for themselves; it discussed in detail not only their goal to prepare the business for sale but also the kind of buyer they would seek, their plans for generating early interest among potential buyers, and so forth. The second plan was for the managers and employees; essentially it was the same business plan minus the details about selling the business.

There was little to gain and much to lose by letting everyone read the same plan. The owners would certainly be doing an admirable job of sharing information. But the managers and employees could be expected to focus inordinately on the plan to sell the business—and the fears and concerns that raised—rather than on the hard work necessary to turn the business around. The business could lose key people who would decide to exit early rather than go through an unsettling business sale, even one that was some years in the future.

The Right Message

The key concern in preparing multiple business plans is making sure that each is tailored to the interests, needs, and fears of its readers. A business plan that is exciting to one group of readers may be terrifying or simply irrelevant to another group.

Consider a business plan for financing. A company wants to raise $3 million and isn't fussy about whether the money comes from a banker or a venture capitalist. Chances are strong, though, that the business plan that appeals to the venture capitalist won't appeal to the banker, and vice versa.

Here's why. The venture capitalist is primarily concerned with the company's market and its growth prospects. The investor wants persuasive evidence that the company's market will be worth at least several hundred million dollars over the next five to ten years and that the company will grow to become a major player in that market—with sales of $50 million to $100 million after five years. In other words, the venture capitalist wants to see strong indications of fast growth. The business plan for this individual should build a solid case for such growth as well as for the management team's ability to handle the growth. That means the company includes not only marketing and sales data but also financial projections that show the impact of rapid growth.

The banker, on the other hand, is concerned mainly with

10

Tailoring the Plan

whether his or her loan will be repaid. The banker will focus on two primary issues: the adequacy of cash flow to cover loan payments and the existence of assets that could be liquidated to repay the loan in the event cash flow turns sour. The banker thus wants to see slow growth rather than fast growth, which could endanger cash flow. The business plan for this individual should emphasize how solid the company is—well established in its marketplace, conservative in its growth plans, and the owner of valuable assets.

The business plan tailored to the venture capitalist would probably scare the living daylights out of the banker. And the one for the banker would probably prompt a yawn and quick rejection from the venture capitalist.

The same point can be applied to other constituencies. New senior managers to whom you plan to make stock options available would probably be most impressed with some combination of the plan for the venture capitalist and banker. Your managers want as much detail and guidance as possible, so they know exactly what's expected of them as well as how they're supposed to fulfill the actual expectations of the targeted readers.

Targeting Your Audience

Most business owners write business plans because they have a specific need that can be met by a particular audience. The owners may need a bank loan. In that case, the business plan will be addressed to bankers. The owners may have decided they need to formalize their company's planning process and require a business plan that all managers can understand.

Sometimes, it's not so simple. Recall the entrepreneur seeking $3 million financing who isn't particular about where the money comes from. While he may not be particular, prospective financiers who read his plan will be very particular about the kind of business they make that kind of money available to.

It will be in this entrepreneur's interests to make a decision early about whether he is targeting venture capitalists or bankers or both. If he is targeting one group, his business plan must be tailored to that group. If he is targeting both, he'd better have two plans.

That targeting becomes important for another reason. When the entrepreneur really thinks about it, he may decide that one or another group of financial backers is preferable for his company's long-term interests. In this case, he'll have to weigh the advantages of giving up a substantial chunk of equity to venture capitalists against the debt burden associated with a large bank loan. He may also want to consider the pros and cons of having a venture capitalist on his board. And he'll want to evaluate the threat associated with a banker that can call the loan at any time.

If you have gone through the analysis described in the previous chapters of this book, these issues will be fairly clear. You will understand not only what you most prefer, but what your company's strengths and weaknesses make feasible.

Targeting Your Plan

Now that you've determined whom you want to address your business plan to, you need to consider what—and how much—that audience really wants to hear. Fred Gibbons of Software Publishing Corp. says that he intentionally kept his business plan to a maximum of ten pages because he knew that venture capitalists appreciate conciseness and brevity. And, indeed, he received compliments (not to mention offers of financing) from each of the three venture capital firms he presented the plan to. He was also able to show the same plan to potential suppliers and key employees because, in addition to being easy to read, it emphasized the company's plans for aggressive sales and marketing that would lead to substantial but controlled growth.

Keep in mind. . . It's possible to have two versions of a plan targeted to the same audience. Some entrepreneurs I know have written a summary plan of 5 to 10 pages and a full plan of 30 to

Business Plan Targeting Summary			
Audience	Issues to emphasize	Issues to deemphasize	Length
Banker	Cash flow, assets, solid growth	Fast growth, hot market	10–20 pp.
Investor	Fast growth, potential large market, management team	Assets	20–40 pp.
Strategic partner	Synergy, proprietary products	Sales force, assets	20–40 pp.
Large customer	Stability, service	Fast growth, hot market	20–40 pp.
Key employees	Security, opportunity	Technology	20–40 pp.
Merger & acquisition	Past accomplishments	Future outlook	20–40 pp.

40 pages. If a banker or investor is intrigued by the more summary plan, the entrepreneur can present the full plan, which contains more detail.

A useful way to evaluate the targeting issue is to compare several likely audiences:

1. Bankers. Bankers are primarily concerned about having their loans repaid. While they will say that they are interested in a company's long-term prospects because they want to establish long-term relationships, bankers want to be assured of a company's ability to keep up a loan repayment schedule. Margins on business loans are so low that banks can't afford to have too many go sour.

Thus, the emphasis should be on cash flow—past, present, and future. The more convincing your past record of cash generation has been, the more likely bankers are to believe future projections. After cash flow, bankers look for tangible assets that can be sold to repay the loan in case cash flow sours. These assets don't have to be limited to those owned by the company.

Indeed, many banks will insist that owners personally guarantee company loans so that if company assets don't cover a loan, the bank can come after the owners' personal property. Thus, the banks may also want a statement covering personal financial assets and liabilities.

Such information can often be covered in a short business plan of 10 to 20 pages.

2. *Investors.* Investors are most interested in factors that can help predict growth, because growth is essential for them to get an attractive return on their investment. These factors include the market's likely future, the management team's experience, evidence of fast-growing sales, and so forth. They want to see their investment go into marketing rather than R&D expenses. The existence of tangible assets is less important to investors because they aren't as concerned with being "repaid" in the same way.

But investors do want to see a concise plan—preferably 40 pages or less.

3. *Strategic partners.* Increasingly, smaller growing companies are seeking out large corporations to provide expansion resources—mainly in the form of investment funds, distribution outlets, and production expertise. Corporate executives have their own agenda. They are most interested in finding new products and/or services that can be integrated into the corporation's existing offerings. Corporate executives also want to secure rights to proprietary products or processes and to emerging technologies. And it helps if the management team has had corporate experience.

Such issues as cash flow and sales-force planning are less important because corporations figure they can compensate for these needs. The business plan should be concise but devote significant detail to the strategic issues of importance to the corporate partner.

10

Tailoring the Plan

4. Large customers. These tend to be major corporations seeking long-term and significant purchasing relationships. The customers want evidence that a smaller company is going to be around to provide not only the product and/or service promised but also warranty or maintenance service.

For these readers, the business plan should emphasize the company's past record of performance and ability to satisfy customers. "Love letters" and names of reference accounts can be especially helpful.

5. Key employees. More than any other single group, potential key employees are looking for reassurance on a variety of issues. They want to know that the company has a history of success and that it can achieve substantial growth in the future. In other words, potential key employees are looking for signs of both security and opportunity, especially if they are going to be getting stock in the company. A business plan that satisfies one of the previously described audiences may well be appropriate for these individuals.

Existing key employees, as noted earlier, want as much detail as possible about the company's plans so that they can determine their individual roles. The more guidance you give them, the more comfortable they will feel.

6. Management team. A business plan intended to guide your company's middle- and upper-level managers usually needs to be more detailed than other plans. As noted in describing the Celestial Seasonings and Pizza Hut plans in Chapters 2 and 3, the managers using the plan want detailed guidance to fulfill the plan's objectives. A plan of 60 pages or more isn't unusual.

7. Merger and acquisition candidates. A company looking to acquire your company is primarily interested in its past and present record of growth and accomplishment. If the acquiring company's executives can be excited about the past and present, they will figure that they can provide input that will solidify the future. Moreover, it's the past record of sales and profits that help determine the company's value. A business plan similar to that submitted to a bank would be useful in this situation.

If your company is doing the acquiring, then the owners of the company you are seeking to buy will want similar data showing that your company has a record of sound accomplishment and seasoned management. In addition, they will want to know as much as possible about the management team of the acquiring company and how it has digested its previous acquisitions.

EXERCISES

Worksheets for this chapter are provided on page 227

1. Identify the target audiences for your business plan.

2. How many variations of the business plan do you need?

3. If you need more than one variation, how will you have to alter the business plan?

10

Tailoring the Plan

Writing and Packaging the Plan: Coming Full Circle

BY NOW, you should have lots of notes and perhaps even drafts of some sections of the plan. The notes come from the information you've been providing in response to the points raised and exercises supplied in previous chapters. The drafts may have come from your first try at an executive summary or from the efforts of your management team to write various chapters.

Chances are, though, that none of that material seems anywhere close to complete. And well it shouldn't as writing is a difficult and demanding task. As I noted at the very beginning of this book, in my experience entrepreneurs become more frustrated with the writing than with any other aspect of the business plan process. As the frustration grows, so do the exasperation and the feelings of incompetence. What started out as a technical problem suddenly becomes a psychological problem.

But that's partly the point. Writing is as much a psychological challenge as it is a technical task. A big part of the challenge lies in getting past the obstacles that your mind places in your way. Many books have been written about effective writing and I won't try to cover that territory here. What I will do in this chapter is offer some observations and pointers about business plan writing, with an eye toward removing the mystery and easing the tension that often surrounds the process.

Writing is a matter of presentation. How the material is organized and looks to the reader helps determine his or her reaction. For that reason, I will include some suggestions for packaging the business plan so it will achieve maximum impact on readers and maximum protection for you and your company.

Observations About Writing

I'm often asked how it is that writing is "so easy" for me, how it is that I can just "turn the copy out" on demand. I have to explain that writing really isn't easy for me or for most professional writers. I can't just turn the copy out on demand.

Just because the final copy turns out well doesn't mean that the process of writing it was easy. Writing is as demanding for professionals as it is for other people for the following three reasons:

1. It's rarely right the first time. There's a perception that good writers sit down at their computers and somehow put together flowing prose at will, on the first try. But most professional writers will tell you that effective written material is rarely produced on the first try. Rather, they will explain, the key to effective writing is frequent rewriting.

Think of other professionals. When we see wonderful gymnasts, ballerinas, or figure skaters, we tend to marvel at how well they perform, ignoring the fact that they've been practicing many hours daily for many years.

Similarly, when we read well-written prose, we tend to assume that it was written that way on the first try and ignore the reality that it probably went through many rewrites or came about as a result of many years spent writing similar material.

2. You can't write in a vacuum. The longer you spend trying to write and rewrite material, the less objective you become. And, indeed, that's one of the main sources of frustration in the writing process. When you write something and get it to the point where you think it's passable and then read it a few hours later and see all kinds of problems, naturally you begin to wonder whether you're really making progress.

That's why you need to have one or two outsiders who know something about business and communication and whose judgment you respect look over your written material from time to time. These individuals can help spot flaws, relieve your frustration, and keep you from spinning your wheels.

Who are these individuals? They may be other business owners or professionals you know, such as accountants or lawyers. If they work in communications fields, such as public relations or promotion, they can also be good evaluators. Of course, if you have business partners, you can help each other in this regard.

3. There's no "right way" to write. Some people do best starting with an outline, which becomes the basis of the written material. Others like to simply plunge in, get a lot down on paper, and then rearrange and rewrite. And others like to begin with handwritten notes on legal paper and then go to the word processor or computer. None of these approaches or their many variations is "better" or more effective than another.

This is an important point to keep in mind because it's easy to get bogged down in a technique that doesn't work for you. If you decide that outlining first is an essential part of the writing process and it doesn't work for you, you'll waste time and get discouraged.

Writing the Business Plan

Once you get yourself past some of the barriers that seem to be an inherent part of the writing process, you can confront some of the issues particular to the business plan. The overriding point, though, is to keep yourself focused as much as possible on business issues rather than on writing issues. My experience is that the better understanding you have of the business issues, the more easily the writing comes.

While there's no one right way to write the business plan (or any other material), here are some approaches/techniques I have found to be useful:

1. Determine the priority of issues/success factors for each area of the business. In other words, for each section of the plan—the company, marketing, product/service, sales, and financial sections—list in order of importance the challenges facing your business. Also provide your approaches/solutions for handling the challenges.

For example, for the sales segment, suppose that key issues are whether you can justify an in-house sales force, how you will train it, and how much advertising you can accomplish within the $10,000 advertising budget you have available. List each of these issues and then explain the justifications or solutions for each. This is how your analysis might look:

> ***Pros of in-house sales force.*** Based on our limited experience, we are confident our salespeople will succeed on one-third of sales calls, making the cost of each sale $600. Manufacturers' reps would cost only $400 in commissions for each sale. But our inability to control the manufacturers' reps makes us uncertain of their ability to generate the sales volume we want to achieve. Our opinion is that the company's long-term interests are better served by the greater likelihood of achieving its sales goals with a costlier in-house sales force than with manufacturers' reps. But to be absolutely certain, we are going to experiment with both, using an in-house sales force for some territories and manufacturers' reps for others on a trial basis.

183

Challenges of training in-house sales force. Similarly, the issue here is one of cost versus control. If we hire our own trainers, our costs will be 25% higher than if we subcontract the training to a company that specializes in providing on-site training. But with an outside firm, we won't have the same control over what's taught as we would with our own people. Once again, we'll experiment with each approach to determine what works best for us.

Such written material—your assessment of the situation—then becomes the basis of the actual plan. More detail will likely be needed comparing costs and other resource issues, but the main issues will be on paper. Once they're on paper, you're in much better shape than if you're staring at a blank page.

2. Include as much supporting material as possible. As you set priorities and list the issues confronting your company, make sure you discuss any experiences you've had or data you've collected that could help in the decision making. It's easy as you move from issue to issue to neglect important supporting information that could make your business plan stronger.

A business plan I read on behalf of a start-up company illustrates what I mean. A woman planning a company that would make and sell a gourmet food product wrote a plan intended to attract investment funds. It provided statistics on the number of gourmet food stores and on growing demand for her type of product and on plans to provide financial incentives to the food stores and so on.

When I met with the woman, I asked her whether she had actually tried to sell her product to any food stores. As a matter of fact, she explained, she had visited some stores and each had expressed a willingness to place a small but not insignificant order for her product to try it out on food shelves. This fact wasn't in the business plan, though. She had forgotten about it.

I asked how many stores she had visited. Only three, she replied. But if she had gotten indications of strong interest from every store she visited, she was doing great, I explained. The favorable feedback from potential buyers of her product was extremely important because it came directly from the market-place. The information and implications belonged in a prominent place in the business plan.

3. Don't make unsupported statements. This is really a variation on the previous point. Don't state opinions as facts, especially when you don't have data to back them up. This is a common problem in many business plans I've seen. Entrepreneurs tend to be optimistic and to treat their upbeat expectations as fact. An expectation that the sales force will succeed in one of every three sales calls can easily become an assertion that the sales force succeeds in one-third of its sales calls.

By going through the process described in this chapter of setting priorities and describing issues, the importance of backing up statements becomes apparent. Failing to provide specifics in answer to questions from a banker or investor about how you can be so sure a particular sales or product approach will work so well is a sure way to undermine confidence in your product.

4. Put one company official in charge of assembling/writing the document. Even if several managers have written chapters, one person needs to rework the material to provide a consistent style and eliminate contradictions and repetitions. That person should be able to write clearly and have the confidence of others he or she is working with; moreover, he or she should be able to handle these responsibilities sensitively and tactfully.

5. Designate an outside reader/editor. After you have worked with a document for a long time period, it becomes nearly impossible to maintain the necessary distance and objec-

tivity to edit effectively. This is especially true for a business plan, which usually evolves over a period of months.

Thus, it is essential that an outsider read through the plan as drafts are completed to find inconsistencies, poor writing, and other problems. As suggested earlier, this person might be an accountant or lawyer or perhaps a business school professor or an individual involved in a communications field like public relations or advertising. The person you choose should have an understanding of business as well as good writing.

You might also want to locate a proofreader to find typos, misspellings, and other minor glitches. They can reflect badly on you and your company.

Packaging Issues

Just as we judge books by their covers and people by the way they dress, so we judge business plans by the way they look. In addition to being clearly and concisely written, the business plan must also be accessible in other ways. The way the plan is bound, typed, and organized sends a message to readers.

At the same time, the plan differs from a book in that it isn't intended for general circulation. Much of the information is confidential, and you don't want it falling into the hands of unauthorized customers, suppliers, or competitors. How you package the plan can affect who it goes to—and doesn't go to.

Here are some suggestions for making the most of your plan's overall appearance:

1. Make it businesslike. The plan should look neither too slick nor too shabby. Too slick could be leather binding and Linotronic typesetting. Too shabby could be faded Xeroxed pages stapled together.

The wonders of desktop publishing have made it possible to put together a business plan that ten years ago would have been considered inordinately fancy. I'm talking about charts and graphs and font varieties that make a plan easy to scan and quickly grasp.

As color printing catches on, I'm certain we'll see the standards for business plans upgraded as they have been for many types of presentations.

2. Look for ways to make the plan stand out. If your plan is going to individuals who tend to see a lot of plans, like bankers or investors, it helps if you can find a way to stand out from the crowd. Undoubtedly, these individuals would welcome a business plan that shows some creativity.

What is a business plan that stands out? It might be one like the owner of a floral business put together, with a cover featuring color photos of cut flowers. Or it might be one like the owner of an electronic components company put together, which contained bulleted single-sentence summaries on the left-hand page to go with the text on the right-hand page. Or one like the owners of a new printing company put together that had photos of various members of the management team included at points where their duties and background were discussed. If the product is small and/or inexpensive enough, you might want to include a sample to accompany the plan.

Increasingly, entrepreneurs seeking financing are including color charts and photos inside the plan to go along with color covers. With the advent of color copiers, it is easy and inexpensive to duplicate color pages.

And more entrepreneurs are including short videos about their companies. For those companies that are well established, the videos might provide glimpses of the company's headquarters and manufacturing operation. For start-up or early-stage companies, the videos might provide brief interviews of the members of the management team summarizing the company's plan.

For potential financial backers, videos provide another dimension to the written plan. Videos give life to the written

11

Writing and Packaging: Coming Full Circle

statements and numbers, enabling the financiers to decide whether they want to go to the next step in the financing process, which is a personal meeting (described in the next section of this chapter).

Getting a video produced can be expensive, especially if it involves many different scenes and interviews and fancy graphics. It isn't unusual for a video to total $1,000 per minute, or $10,000 for a ten-minute video. One that simply includes two or three top executives summarizing segments of the plan would likely cost much less. Also, it's sometimes possible to negotiate barter or other such arrangements with individual video producers to keep out-of-pocket expenses down.

3. Tend to the details. As noted in Chapter 2, that means a cover page with the company's phone number and a table of contents with page numbers. It also means that the plan has been carefully proofread for typos and misspellings. These little things, if not tended to, can easily turn off potential backers.

4. Limit access. While you want the plan to be attractive and accessible, you don't want it going to anyone besides those individuals for whom it is intended. Here are three ways you can limit its circulation:

• *Number the plans.* Each plan should have its own number—shown on the cover page—preferably below 10 or 12, to convey the message that the plan has been duplicated in small numbers and that each plan's reader is known and accounted for.

• *Include a statement that copying is prohibited.* On the cover page or table of contents, include a sentence or two to this effect: "The contents of this plan are proprietary and confidential. It is not to be copied or duplicated in any way."

• *Insist that readers sign a confidentiality statement.* This is a simple statement in which readers agree to refrain from revealing the plan's contents or ideas to anyone else. (Exhibit 11–1 shows a copy of a sample confidentiality agreement.)

Keep in mind. . . None of the steps just discussed guarantees that the plan won't be copied and read by others. But they will likely inhibit most of those who read your plan from simply running it through a copying machine and handing it out. It will also inhibit them from freely discussing the plan's contents with others.

Personally Presenting the Plan

If you're using your plan to try to raise cash, you may be called upon to present your business plan personally to bankers or investors. In this event, be prepared to impress your audience. Many of the same rules that apply to preparing the business plan also apply to a personal presentation. Here are those I have found to be most important:

1. Keep it short and to the point. Unless you're told otherwise, your presentation should be kept to half an hour or less. Like the written plan, the presentation should be concise and easy to understand. That means extracting the most important points from the plan and running through them in an interesting and logical way.

2. Use visual aids. These may be slides or overhead transparencies. They may simply state points from the plan in a phrase or two. But in our visually oriented society, they help keep your audience focused on the important points.

3. Involve several members of your management team. If you have a marketing manager and a financial executive, allow each of them to speak for five minutes or so. This not only breaks things up, but conveys the impression that your company consists of more than just you.

4. Try to demonstrate your product or service. If possible, bring a sample that listeners can hold and touch or watch being

189

demonstrated. One of the best examples of a service demonstration I saw was for a company that put on dramatic presentations for corporate organizations. The company performed a skit in which one of the characters was nearly murdered—to convey the excitement of the service the company sells. Following the short skit, the company president presented the business details to a rapt audience.

In Sum

Because writing is as much art as science, there isn't a proven formula for guaranteeing its success. My concluding advice to business owners trying to become better writers is to keep it simple. Write in short sentences. Don't get bogged down in technical details. And do lots of rewriting.

EXERCISES

Worksheets for this chapter are provided on page 228

1. Select the person in your company who will oversee preparation of the business plan.

2. Select an outsider who will periodically review the plan for consistency and accuracy.

3. Put together a 30-minute oral presentation of your business plan with accompanying visual aids.

EXHIBIT 11-1:

CONFIDENTIALITY STATEMENT

XYZ Inc.
100 Main Street
Anytown, Mass.

[Date]

ABC Investments
101 Main Street
Anytown, Mass.

Attention: _____

Gentlemen:

You and XYZ, Inc. (the "Company") have entered into this Agreement to define your responsibilities with respect to information received and to be received from the Company in the course of discussions about your possible participation in a proposed investment in the Company.

1. All information given to you about the Company by the Company, including but not limited to the Company's Business Plan dated _____, and any updates thereto, shall be deemed to be "Confidential Information" for purposes of this Agreement.

2. You shall not use or disclose any of the Confidential Information without the Company's prior written permission, except for information which, when you received it, was well known to you as evidenced by prior written materials or publications.

3. You also agree that as long as this Agreement is in effect and for one year thereafter, you will not directly or indirectly, either alone or with one or more parties, seek to acquire or invest in the Company, without the prior written consent of the Company.

4. You agree that you will not, without the prior written permission of the Company, use the Confidential Information for any purpose other than that required for the discussions hereunder. You represent that you have no obligations or commitments inconsistent with this Agreement. You agree to limit disclosure of Confidential Information received hereunder to only those of your officers and employees who are directly concerned with the discussions between you and the Company. You shall advise your officers and employees of the proprietary nature of the Confidential Information and shall use all reasonable safeguards to prevent the unauthorized disclosure of such Confidential Information by them.

5. Nothing contained in this Agreement shall require either party to enter into any future agreement with the other. Upon termination of the discussions hereunder, you shall promptly return all materials containing Confidential Information, including all extracts and copies thereof, to the Company.

6. You agree that the remedy at law of the Company would be inadequate as to any unauthorized use or disclosure of the Confidential Information by you and agree that the Company shall be entitled to preliminary and permanent injunctions in any court of competent jurisdiction to prevent such unauthorized use or disclosure by you.

7. This Agreement shall be construed and enforced in accordance with and governed by the laws of the commonwealth of Massachusetts, which shall be the sole venue for resolution of any dispute arising under this Agreement.

8. This Agreement, including any term hereof, may be amended or terminated only in writing by the parties hereto.

9. This agreement embodies the entire agreement and understanding between the parties with respect to the subject matter hereof and supersedes all prior agreements and understandings relating to the subject matter hereof.

10. All of the terms of this Agreement, whether so expressed or not, shall be binding upon the respective successors and assigns of the parties hereto and shall inure to the benefit of and be enforceable by the parties hereto and their respective successors and assigns.

Please indicate your acknowledgment and acceptance of the terms of this Agreement by executing the enclosed duplicate original of this Agreement and returning it to the Company.

XYZ, INC.

By:

Name and Title

ACKNOWLEDGED AND ACCEPTED:

By:

Name and Title

(Provided courtesy of the law firm of O'Connor, Broude, Snyder & Aronson, Waltham, Mass.)

PART FOUR:
CONCLUSION

Making the Plan
Work for You

O K, YOU'VE written your plan. It's in the hands of bankers or your operating managers and, if all goes well, is serving its intended purpose. What's next?

Before I attempt to answer that question, I think it's important to reflect a bit. Written business plans, broadly speaking, are usually put together for either of two purposes: to prepare for a significant event, such as obtaining financing, or to guide the company's operations for a particular period, usually a year.

It's important to keep these two purposes in mind as we draw to the end of this book and consider how you can make the most of your business plan. If the plan is intended to secure financing, a successful plan gets the ball rolling, leading to discussion and negotiations.

If the plan is intended to guide the company's operations for a year, then a decision must be made about what to do about the plan after a year. If the plan has been judged useful, then company executives are inclined to revise and rewrite the plan for the following year.

In either case, it's important to remember a fundamental

fact about business plans: *business plans become outdated very rapidly and, if not updated, lose whatever value they may have to a company.* In other words, business planning is an ongoing process and the written plan must be regularly revised if it is going to have continuing value.

More often than not, executives of new and growing companies write a single plan and then breathe a big sigh of relief. They're done. But in several respects, both philosophical and practical, they've only just begun.

Keeping Up with Change

The reality of today's world is that the pace of change is accelerating. What that means is that executives must be constantly making adjustments to their plans. As the pace of change speeds up, it is easy to lose sight of the business plan and simply make the necessary adjustments to the plan on a day-to-day basis.

I do not mean to suggest that the plan must be adjusted in writing on a daily or even a weekly basis. But I do believe it is essential to review the plan on at least a quarterly basis and measure results against the plan.

One way to accomplish this task without being under the pressure of completely rewriting the plan each quarter is to establish priorities and implementation steps as part of the planning and quarterly review process. Thus, if the company is contemplating three selling methods, priorities should be attached to each of the three. One selling method might be made a high priority, the second a medium priority, and a third a low priority.

Another way to help the review and measurement process is to set target dates for completing various components of the plan. In establishing a new-product development process, dates should be established for major milestones.

The priorities and dates can be included at the end of each section of the plan or in a separate section at the end of the completed plan. In either case, they should be taken very seriously if they are to have the intended effect of helping in the plan review process. Deadlines have a way of slipping in many companies; simply pushing the dates back a few months at each quarterly review quickly renders the whole process meaningless.

Executives and other employees must be judged on their ability to meet the plan's deadlines. If adjustments or delays are necessary for valid operational or planning reasons, these must be discussed and analyzed.

As the priorities and dates are examined and discussed, the necessity for making changes in the overall plan will become clear. It may be that the priorities should be changed after six months and a high-priority selling method is judged to be inappropriate. In that case, the section on selling and promotion may need to be revised to explain the change in priorities.

With word processing and spreadsheets so accessible, such adjustments aren't as big a deal as they might once have been. What is key to the success of such ongoing changes is that they be transmitted to the executives who need to implement the changes—and not simply be kept on the computer of the chief executive doing the fine-tuning.

1. Negotiating: How Solid Are Your Projections?

If your plan is intended to help your company raise money, you will almost certainly come under questioning and scrutiny from the financiers. How can you be so sure that you will achieve the market penetration you project? Have you given enough credence to the competitive pressures you'll encounter? Aren't you perhaps underestimating your sales and administrative expenses? How certain are you that you'll collect 60% of your receivables in 30 days? And on and on.

Some of the questions and criticisms you encounter will be sincere concerns based on the battle-hardened inquirers' previous experiences with smaller growing companies. Some, though, will be negotiating ploys. The amount of financing a

12

banker or investor is willing to commit is linked to his or her assessment of the plan's overall credibility.

In certain instances, the business plan's projections may affect negotiations. If you are seeking funds to provide essential cash to carry you through a growth spurt, financiers will see in your plan the potential impact on the company of a failure to raise the funds. They will also be well aware that if certain assumptions made in the plan don't work out, your company's situation could be even more desperate. Venture capitalists, in particular, have been known to let negotiations drag out intentionally in the expectation that entrepreneurs will become increasingly desperate to make a deal.

Of course, the more solid a case your plan makes, and the stronger your negotiating stance, the better your chances of getting what you want. Your success depends partly on what you are seeking from financial backers. And partly it depends on hooking up with the most appropriate financiers.

In the case of Software Publishing, Fred Gibbons was looking for $250,000 of investment in exchange for 25% of the company. That meant he was asking the backers to accept a $1-million valuation of the company. The plan he wrote made an extremely convincing case. Clearly he matched up well with the financial types because he had offers from three venture capital firms for funding and selected the one he liked best.

The venture capitalists, of course, knew what they were doing. The company by 1989 had a value in the public markets of $250 million, making that 25% stake acquired for $250,000 worth $65 million. "That's a 250-to-1 return, which by Silicon Valley standards is phenomenal," says Gibbons. "A 10-to-1 return is a good base hit and a 100-to-1 return is a home run."

Keep in mind. . . You don't have a deal with bankers or investors until you've signed a final agreement and received a check. No matter how strong the expression of interest or support you get from potential backers, keep as many options open as long as possible. There's nothing wrong with negotiating two or three deals at once, so if something falls through, you'll still have alternatives.

2. Making the Plan: What's Realistic?

When you think about it, the proof of the pudding as far as any business plan is concerned is how it compares with reality. Investors and bankers will tell you that in their experience, entrepreneurs are lucky to achieve half the sales and profits their plans project.

Indeed, financiers customarily "discount" the plan's projections to a certain level in determining the amount of financing to make available. That is, bankers may discount the value of assets or receivables intended as collateral. Venture capitalists may discount the expected sales and profits, which are used to help determine the company's future value, as a way to gauge how much of the company they get for how much investment.

For an operating plan, achieving only half the expected results is clearly not acceptable. That's because an operating plan, if it is truly being relied on by managers, is guiding the spending, hiring, and other decisions. If those decisions are being implemented according to plan, while sales and profits are coming in at only 50% of expectations, serious problems will occur.

How the successful companies did. The entrepreneurs whose plans we have examined in this book have all been remarkably successful in setting and even surpassing their projections. Those seeking financing defied the conventional wisdom about business plans. Software Publishing more than doubled its projected sales. People Express eclipsed its plan within a matter of months in terms of its expected capacity and, when it opened for business, in terms of revenues. Ben and Jerry's came in ahead of expectations as well.

The operating plans of Celestial Seasonings and Pizza Hut

12

Making the Plan Work for You

199

were also consistently within 10% of target. As I've pointed out before, the accuracy of operating plans is more than an academic matter, for obvious reasons. But there's more to it than simply making sure there are enough sales to support the employees you have.

Staying on target. According to Mo Siegel of Celestial Seasonings, there's an inherent tension in the process of setting goals for an operating plan. "Ideally, we should be at about 85% of target," he explains. "If we hit every one of our objectives, we're not pushing hard enough. If we're lower than 85%, we're bad planners and dreamers."

How can companies ensure that their plans stay close to reality? At Celestial Seasonings, says Siegel, "We reviewed the plan quarterly. And I had every officer bonused on the sales and profit objectives. At the end of each year, we did a performance review: how people did versus what they said they'd do. And we had a score." In other words, there was accountability.

Celestial Seasonings met or exceeded its plan most years, because of the special emphasis given to gap planning (described in Chapter 3), notes Siegel.

3. The Follow-up: What Do You Do, Or Not Do, for an Encore?

As I suggested at the beginning of this chapter, most entrepreneurs have a very specific purpose for their business plan and, once that purpose has been accomplished, the formal planning process is over. The People Express business plan is the only written plan the company ever put together. The question of why the company never assembled another plan to guide its astonishing growth is one that prompts extensive explanation from founder Donald Burr.

Quite simply, he begins, the company didn't really need an operating plan once it had financial backing. Not even for budgeting purposes?

"We felt budgeting was one of the things that stand in the

way of customer service," he explains. "The mind-set of budgeting is that it's finance driven instead of customer driven."

Burr points to Continental Airlines, which acquired People Express, to illustrate his point. "Continental Airlines lives by budgeting," he says. "From the food to the uniforms to the people, it's budget driven. You end up with a seriously flawed product as a result of such a process."

As for People Express, he explains, "We figured out what we wanted to do as we went along. You have to hire people and buy equipment and everything else goes along. We focused everything on the equipment and operations of the company. We had a very low-cost system. We did not spend any money on engineering."

He acknowledges the criticism of People Express as a company lacking the controls or other discipline that an ongoing business plan might have helped bring about and he is unimpressed. "I've heard all the criticism about arrogance and no controls and distractions from acquisitions," he says. "People Express was more in control than any airline."

Tracing the downfall. Why, then, did People Express sell out to Texas Air under the pressure of heavy losses six years after start-up? That had nothing to do with planning, or lack thereof, Burr maintains.

The problem, he argues, came from "the technological change in the industry." The change became apparent in early 1985, when American Airlines inaugurated a computerized distribution system that enabled the airline to track competing airlines' prices and match or beat them, sometimes within hours of implementation. "They changed their prices by the minute," he recalls. "We could never tell what they were doing."

Until that time, notes Burr, "We could never satisfy demand. But then they [competitors] said, 'We'll sell you a seat at their price or less.' "

The meaning: "They had a better product at a lower price,"

Burr says. "We were lucky to be able to sell the airline to Texas Air."

Wouldn't the exercise of putting together a business plan have enabled the company to anticipate the impact of competitors making use of the information revolution? Not surprisingly, Burr is negative. The efforts by competitors weren't a total surprise, he says. "We had decided early on that we couldn't afford the billion dollars to have a competitive information system," he explains. "So we had none.

"We raised $1 billion [for equipment]," he explains. "We couldn't raise another $1 billion for an information system."

A counterargument. But even if Burr were aware of competitors' efforts to use information for competitive advantage, he admits he was caught off guard by the huge impact the effort had on his company. "We were producing American Airlines' product for $1 billion a year less than it was," he recalls. "We were feared. They put us out of business in nine months. We were a healthy, profitable company. In nine months, they broke us."

In that last statement, I would argue, Burr makes the strongest case possible for a formal planning approach. Had top executives of the company been involved in planning, they would have been examining closely their competitors' marketing approaches. People Express officials would have been considering their own company's strengths and weaknesses in that light and possibly have recognized earlier the tremendous potential impact of information technology. They might well have made a different decision about allocating their resources to establish an information base—or they may have become involved in a joint venture to accomplish the same goal at a lower cost.

Planning doesn't ensure success. But it reduces the chances of surprises of the sort that caught People Express off guard.

In Conclusion

I don't want to get preachy about the importance of planning. Let me simply say that for planning to work in an ongoing way, it has to be part of an ongoing process.

Moreover, I believe it's fair to say that the first business plan is invariably the toughest. Which suggests that the process and the writing all get easier (though "easier" used in a relative sense, since writing a business plan is never easy).

My point is that once you've done a first plan, don't be so quick to discard the process. Let it work for you. It may not always feel good, but it's invariably good for your business.

12

Making the Plan
Work for You

EXERCISES

EXERCISES

To get you started in the planning process, here are two exercises. The first is a quiz and the second is a writing assignment.

I. Quiz   **a.**   **b.**

1. Which do you prefer?
   a. Personally making your business's
      product or fulfilling its service.
   b. Getting others to do the work.   _____   _____

2. What kind of organization interests you more?
   a. A small, stable organization
   b. A fast-growing organization with lots
      of new people and new assignments   _____   _____

3. Which approach to work gives you the most satisfaction?
   a. Doing detailed tasks such as
      personally keeping the books.
   b. Making strategic decisions but
      getting others to execute them.   _____   _____

4. Which leadership style best describes you?
   a. Like to be in charge of the business.
   b. Am willing to share authority
      with others.   _____   _____

5. Which of these business goals are most important to you?
   a. Achieving the freedom and
      independence of being the owner.
   b. Gaining the satisfaction of seeing
      the organization grow and expand.   _____   _____

6. Which of the following financial goals is
   most important to you?
   a. Making a good living from the
      business within three years.
   b. Making a marginal living from
      the business for several years, with
      the prospect of becoming a
      millionaire in seven to ten years.   _____   _____

a.   b.

7. How do you feel about hiring and motivating people?
    a. It's one of the business task
       an owner has to endure.
    b. It's one of the great challenges
       and sources of excitement
       in running a business.   _____   _____

TOTAL As AND Bs   _____   _____

If you picked five or more "a" answers, you're a good candidate for a lifestyle business. If you picked five or more "b" answers, you're a good candidate for a high-flyer business.

II. Writing Assignment

Describe in 50 words or less your principal personal goals in starting, operating, or expanding your business.

_____

_____

_____

_____

_____

_____

_____

_____

_____

_____

_____

_____

EXERCISES

As you come to some decisions about which of these three types of business plans you will write, do the following:

1. ***Begin mapping a table of contents.*** *Consider what subjects must be covered in your plan. Evaluate the subject areas listed earlier in this chapter and decide how you should cover them in your business plan. What particular areas must be added to allow you to discuss the special aspects of your industry, as in the People Express model?*

_____

_____

_____

_____

_____

_____

_____

_____

_____

_____

_____

_____

_____

_____

_____

_____

_____

_____

_____

2. ***Start to make notes under each subject of your contents.***
Now, list the subject areas again, and make a few notes about issues you want to be sure to cover, such as names of competitors (in the section on marketing) or your arguments for having an in-house sales force (in the section on sales).

_____

_____

_____

_____

_____

_____

_____

_____

_____

_____

_____

_____

_____

_____

_____

_____

_____

_____

_____

_____

EXERCISES

1. Based on the stage of your business and the management team in place, determine who will be involved in drafting and finalizing the business plan.

_____

_____

_____

_____

_____

2. Set aside time for the people involved to write and discuss the business plan.

_____

_____

_____

_____

_____

3. Based on the complexity of your business, set a maximum length for the business plan.

_____

_____

_____

_____

_____

_____

_____

_____

_____

_____

EXERCISES The four executive summaries found on pages 62-66 are composites based on real executive summaries. Read each carefully, and then answer the following questions:

1. Which two are the most effective executive summaries?

_____

_____

_____

_____

_____

_____

2. Which two are the least effective executive summaries?

_____

_____

_____

_____

_____

3. In the best executive summaries, describe the three most important strengths.

_____

_____

_____

_____

_____

_____

_____

4. In the worst executive summaries, list the three most significant weaknesses.

_____

_____

_____

_____

_____

_____

_____

_____

_____

_____

5. What would you do to strengthen the worst ones?

_____

_____

_____

_____

_____

_____

_____

_____

_____

_____

EXERCISES

1. Describe in five sentences or less your company's strategy for the previous three years.

   _____

   _____

   _____

   _____

   _____

   _____

   _____

   _____

   _____

   _____

   _____

2. Define your company's mission in three sentences or less.

   _____

   _____

   _____

   _____

   _____

   _____

   _____

   _____

   _____

   _____

3. Explain realistically, in a few paragraphs, how your company's management team will achieve its strategy.

_____

_____

_____

_____

_____

_____

_____

_____

_____

_____

_____

_____

_____

_____

_____

_____

_____

_____

_____

_____

_____

4. Explain in a few paragraphs how your company plans to use technology and manage information to improve the likelihood of overall success.

_____

_____

_____

_____

_____

_____

_____

_____

_____

_____

_____

_____

_____

_____

_____

_____

_____

_____

_____

_____

_____

5. If a conflict exists between your company's strategy, mission, and technology plans and its past accomplishments, how will you deal with the inconsistency?

_____

_____

_____

_____

_____

_____

_____

_____

_____

_____

_____

_____

_____

_____

_____

_____

_____

_____

_____

_____

_____

_____

_____

CHAPTER SIX

EXERCISES

1. List your product's or service's three principal customer benefits.

   _____

   _____

   _____

   _____

   _____

   _____

2. Identify three sources of market research.

   _____

   _____

   _____

3. Identify your top two competitors and explain the primary strengths and weaknesses of each.

   _____

   _____

   _____

   _____

   _____

   _____

   _____

   _____

   _____

   _____

   _____

4. Describe at least two ways in which your company will gain a competitive advantage over the top competitors you have identified.

_____

_____

_____

_____

_____

_____

_____

_____

_____

_____

_____

_____

_____

_____

_____

_____

_____

_____

_____

_____

_____

_____

EXERCISES

1. List the four most important features of your company's main product or service.

_____

_____

_____

_____

_____

_____

2. List the four least important features of your company's main product or service.

_____

_____

_____

_____

_____

3. Determine which of the least important features is most costly. How necessary is that feature?

_____

_____

_____

_____

_____

_____

4. Relate in three or four sentences how your company would respond if demand for your company's product or service exceeded your expectations.

_____

_____

_____

_____

_____

_____

_____

_____

_____

_____

5. Describe in three or four sentences your company's plans for providing after-sales service.

_____

_____

_____

_____

_____

_____

_____

_____

_____

_____

CHAPTER EIGHT

EXERCISES

1. Determine an alternative sales distribution approach to the one you use or are planning to use and document its feasibility for adding to sales.

_____

_____

_____

_____

_____

_____

_____

_____

_____

_____

2. Identify three publications that could publish articles about your company and provide subjects and approaches for getting the articles published.

_____

_____

_____

_____

_____

_____

_____

_____

_____

3. Identify three sources for "love letters" that you can include in your business plan.

_____

_____

_____

_____

_____

_____

_____

_____

_____

_____

_____

_____

_____

_____

_____

_____

_____

_____

_____

_____

_____

_____

_____

EXERCISES

1. Here is important financial data necessary to construct a cash flow statement for the ABC Personnel Agency:

    January 1, cash on hand was $48,000.
    Income from client billings was as follows:
    January: $36,000
    February: $30,000
    March: $28,000
    April: $28,000
    Expenditures for the company, $496,500/year, as follows:
    Annual Salaries (including fringe benefits):
    President: $100,000
    Senior Vice-President: $70,000
    Vice-President: $48,000
    Office Manager: $42,000
    2 Placement Counselors: $36,000
    2 Associate Placement Counselors: $30,000
    2 Trainees: $24,000
    2 Secretaries: $20,000
    Other expenses:
    Rent: $52,000
    Utilities: $6,000
    Phone: $6,000
    Professional services (accounting, legal): $15,000
    Sales expenses (travel and entertainment): $24,000
    Supplies and forms: $12,000
    Furniture and equipment: $6,000
    Bank debt service (11% on $50,000 credit line): $5,500

2. Construct a cash flow statement for ABC Personnel Agency for the first four months of the year.

ABC PERSONNEL SERVICES				
MONTHLY CASH FLOW STATEMENT ($000)				
MONTH	Jan.	Feb.	March	April
ITEM				

a. What is the trend of the cash flow over the year?

_____

_____

_____

_____

_____

_____

_____

_____

_____

_____

b. Does this trend present any potential problem? If so, what steps might the company take to correct the situation?

_____

_____

_____

_____

_____

_____

_____

_____

_____

(After working out a statement, compare your results with those in Exercise 9-A.)

EXERCISES

1. Identify the target audiences for your business plan.

    _____

    _____

    _____

    _____

    _____

    _____

2. How many variations of the business plan do you need?

    _____

    _____

3. If you need more than one variation, how will you have to alter the business plan?

    _____

    _____

    _____

    _____

    _____

    _____

    _____

    _____

    _____

    _____

    _____

CHAPTER ELEVEN

EXERCISES

1. Select the person in your company who will oversee final preparation of the business plan.

_____

_____

_____

2. Select an outsider who will periodically review the plan for consistency and accuracy.

_____

_____

_____

3. Put together a 30-minute oral presentation of your business plan with accompanying visual aids.

_____

_____

_____

_____

_____

_____

_____

_____

_____

_____

_____

_____

INDEX